Show me

1-2-3® for Windows™

Sherry Kinkoph

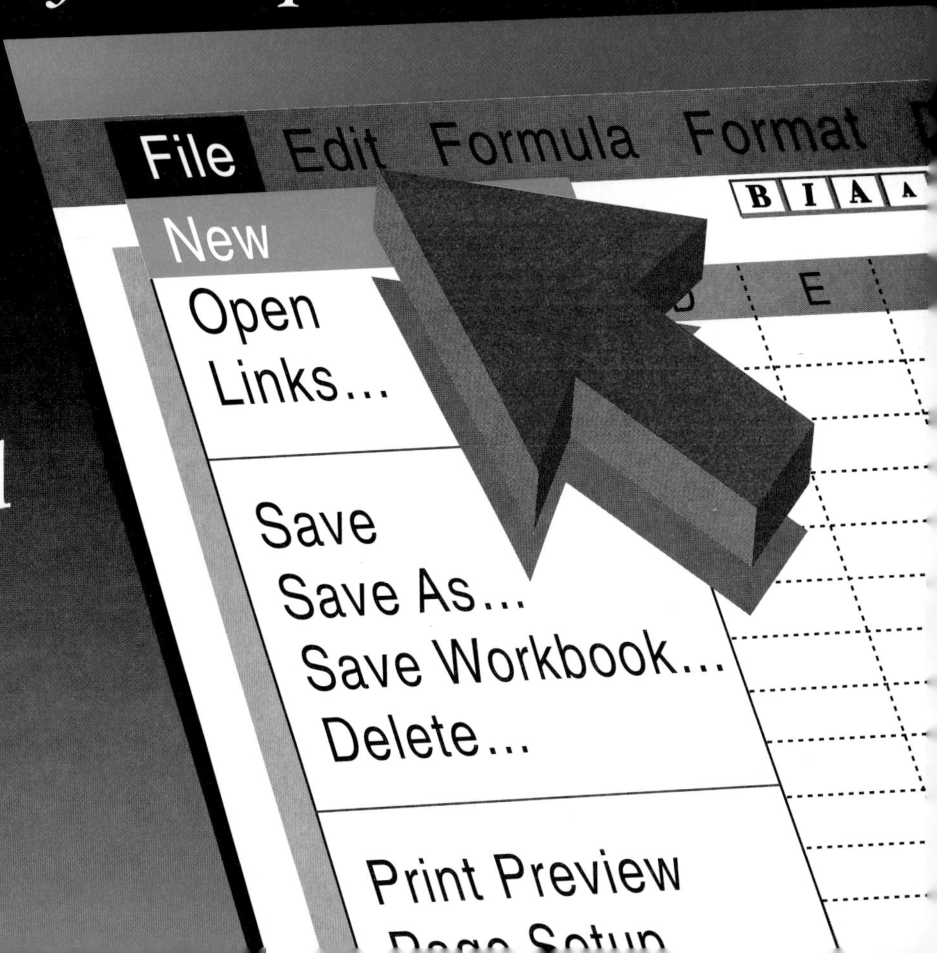

MW00906206

Read less—
learn faster

Easy, illustrated
steps

alpha books

File	Edit	Formula	Format

B I A A

New

Open
Links...

Save
Save As...
Save Workbook...
Delete...

Print Preview

International Standard Book Number: 1-56761-402-7
Library of Congress Catalog Card Number: 93-73708

95 94 93   9 8 7 6 5 4 3 2

Interpretation of the printing code: the rightmost number of the first series of numbers is the year of the book's printing; the rightmost number of the second series of numbers is the number of the book's printing. For example, a printing code of 93-1 shows that the first printing of the book occurred in 1993.

Screen reproductions in this book were created by means of the program Collage Plus from Inner Media, Inc., Hollis, NH.

Printed in the United States of America

TRADEMARKS

Publisher   *Marie Butler-Knight*
Managing Editor   *Elizabeth Keaffaber*
Product Development Manager   *Faithe Wempen*
Acquisitions Manager   *Barry Pruett*
Development Editors   *Seta Frantz*
Manuscript Editor   *San Dee Phillips*
Cover Design   *Scott Fulmer*
Interior Design   *Roger Morgan*
Index   *Jennifer Eberhardt*
Production   *Katy Bodenmiller, Diana Bigham-Griffin, Kim Cofer, Jenny Kucera, Beth Rago, Greg Simsic*

Special Thanks to C. Herbert Feltner for ensuring the technical accuracy

CONTENTS

Introduction 1

Part 1 Basic 1-2-3 for Windows Tasks   11

Starting Windows 12

Starting 1-2-3 13

Understanding the 1-2-3 Screen....................................15

Using 1-2-3 Menus 17

Working with Dialog Boxes 20

Working with SmartIcons 22

Moving and Hiding SmartIcons......................................24

Getting Help from 1-2-3 27

Understanding the Worksheet Structure..........................29

Moving Around the Worksheet Window 30

Adding New Worksheets to a Worksheet File...................33

Viewing Multiple Worksheets in a Worksheet File 36

Exiting 1-2-3 38

Part 2 Creating and Saving Worksheets   39

Entering Data 40

Selecting Ranges...46

Naming Ranges...49

Entering Formulas 52

Using Operators and Operator Precedence.....................55

Understanding Relative and Absolute Cell Referencing ...57

Using Built-In Functions 59

Saving a Worksheet...63

Part 3 Editing and Printing   67

Editing Data...68

Moving and Copying Data...71

Opening a Worksheet 75

Closing a Worksheet..77

Using Print Preview 78

Printing a Worksheet 80

Page Setup Options 82

Part 4 Formatting Your Worksheet   83

Formatting Data...84

Working with Fonts 88

Changing Column Width and Row Height 91

Adding Borders 95

Working with Styles 98

Part 5 Beyond the Basics   101

Creating a Chart 102

Moving and Resizing a Chart..107

Adding Chart Enhancements..110

Changing a Chart's Axis...113

Using Graphics 117

Creating a Database...123

Sorting a Database 126

Searching a Database..128

Installation   131

Glossary   135

Index   137

INTRODUCTION

Have you ever said to yourself, "I wish someone would just *show me* how to use 1-2-3 for Windows." If you have, this *Show Me* book is for you. In it, you won't find detailed explanations of what's going on in your computer each time you enter a command. Instead, you will see pictures that *show you*, step-by-step, how to perform a particular task.

This book will make you feel as though you have your very own personal trainer standing next to you, pointing at the screen and showing you exactly what to do.

WHAT IS LOTUS 1-2-3 FOR WINDOWS 4.0?

So what exactly is Lotus 1-2-3 for Windows 4.0? It is a spreadsheet program designed to help you work with numbers and other data in an organized worksheet format. Worksheets can be anything that contain data: a sales report, a budget analysis with charts, a database table of addresses, and more.

Most of the time, we'll just call the product 1-2-3 rather than using the full name "Lotus 1-2-3 for Windows 4.0." Since 1-2-3 is a Windows-based product, it's designed to be used from within another program, Microsoft Windows. If you're not familiar with Windows, don't worry—this book will ease you into it.

Spreadsheet programs, such as 1-2-3 for Windows 4.0, come with a huge assortment of features to dress up your worksheet data. In addition to the basics of entering data, making corrections, and printing out your results, you can:

- Use built-in functions to perform complex calculations.

- Save time with SmartIcons, buttons that help you get things done fast.

- Add borders, fonts, and styles to make your data look great.

- Work on more than one worksheet at the same time.

- Display information in charts and graphs.

- Preview and fine-tune your worksheet before you print it.

What Does 1-2-3 Look Like?

1-2-3 looks a lot like other Windows-based programs you may have seen. (If you haven't seen a Windows-based program before, that's okay.) The main screen is a rectangular window. The text you type appears in the middle, and around the edges are buttons, menus, borders, and other items that help you control 1-2-3.

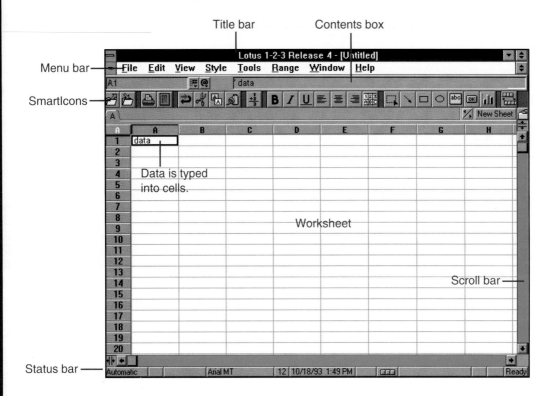

Don't worry about memorizing the parts of the window now; you'll learn more about them later in the book.

HOW TO USE THIS BOOK

Using this book is as simple as falling off your chair. Just flip to the task that you want to perform, and follow the steps. You will see easy step-by-step instructions that tell you which keys to press and which commands to select. You will also see step-by-step pictures that show you what to do. Follow the steps or the pictures (or both) to complete the task. Here's an example of a set of instructions from this book.

Saving a Worksheet

1 Click on **File**, or press **Alt+F**.

2 Click on Save **As**, or press **A**.

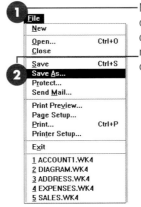

Numbered steps on the left side will correspond to the numbers shown on the figures.

3 Enter the worksheet name in the File **n**ame box.

4 If desired, select drive, directory, and file type options.

5 Click on **OK**, or press **Enter**.

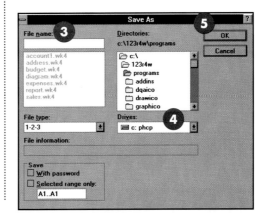

Every computer book has its own way of telling you which buttons to push and which keys to press. Here's how this book handles those formalities:

- Keys that you should press are printed in **boldface type** and appear as they do on your keyboard (for example, press **Alt** or press **F10**). If you need to press more than one key at once, the keys are separated with plus signs. For example, if the text tells you to press **Alt+F**, hold down the **Alt** key while pressing the **F** key.

- Text that you should type is printed in **boldface type like this**.

- Some features are activated by selecting a menu and then a command. If I tell you to "select **File New**," you should open the **File** menu and select the **New** command. In this book, the selection letter is printed in boldface for easy recognition.

Definitions in Plain English

In addition to the basic step-by-step approach, pages may contain Learn the Lingo definitions to help you understand key terms. These definitions are placed off to the side, so you can easily skip them.

LEARNING THE LINGO

Pull-down menu: A menu that appears at the top of the screen, listing various commands. The menu is not visible until you select it from the menu bar. The menu then drops down, covering a small part of the screen.

Quick Refreshers

If you need to know how to perform some other task in order to perform the current task, look for a Quick Refresher. With the Quick Refresher, you won't have to flip through the book to learn how to perform the other task; the information is right where you need it.

QUICK REFRESHER

Making dialog box selections

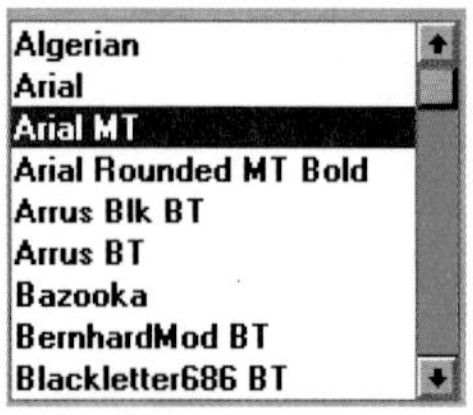
Algerian
Arial
Arial MT
Arial Rounded MT Bold
Arrus Blk BT
Arrus BT
Bazooka
BernhardMod BT
Blackletter686 BT

List box. Click on a list item to choose it. Use the scroll bar to view additional items.

Color:

Drop-down list. Click on the down arrow to the right of the list to display it. Click on the desired item.

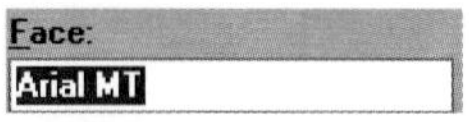
Face:
Arial MT

Text box. Click to place the I-beam in the box. Type your entry.

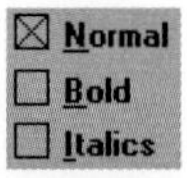
Normal
Bold
Italics

Check box. Click on a box to select or deselect it. (You can select more than one.)

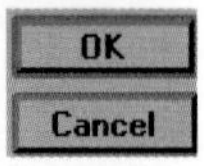
OK
Cancel

Command button. Click on a button to execute the command. (All dialog boxes have at least two command buttons: OK to execute your selections, and Cancel to cancel the selections.)

Tips, Ideas, and Shortcuts

Throughout this book, you will encounter tips that provide important information about a task or tell you how to perform the task more quickly.

Exercises

Because most people learn by doing, several exercises throughout the book give you additional practice performing a task.

Exercise

Type in the text shown and follow the steps below to practice changing alignment for each cell. Remember to select each cell first.

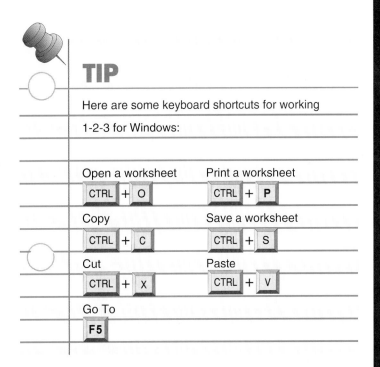

1 Click on **Style** or press **Alt+S**, and then click on **Alignment** or press **A**.

2 When the Alignment dialog box appears, turn on the Horizontal option button that corresponds with the text position you typed in for that cell. To turn on an option, click the box beside the option name, or type the selection letter.

3 Click on **OK**, or press **Enter** to exit the dialog box.

4 Repeat steps 1–3 for each cell that you are aligning.

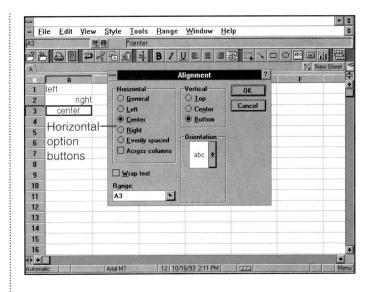

Where Should You Start?

If this is your first encounter with computers, read the next section, "Quick Computer Tour," before reading anything else. This section explains some computer basics that you need to know in order to get your computer up and running.

Once you know the basics, you can work through this book from beginning to end or skip around from task to task, as needed. If you decide to skip around, there are several ways you can find what you're looking for:

- Use the Table of Contents at the front of this book to find a specific task you want to perform.

- Use the complete Index at the back of this book to look up a specific task or topic and find the page number on which it is covered.

- Use the color-coded sections to find groups of related tasks.

- Flip through the book, and look at the task titles at the top of the pages. This method works best if you know the general location of the task in the book.

- Use the inside back cover of this book to quickly find the page on which a command you are looking for is covered.

QUICK COMPUTER TOUR

If this is your first time in front of a computer, the next few sections will teach you the least you need to know to get started.

Parts of a Computer

Think of a computer as a car. The system unit holds the engine that powers the computer. The monitor is like the windshield that lets you see where you're going. And the keyboard and mouse are like the steering wheel, which allow you to control the computer.

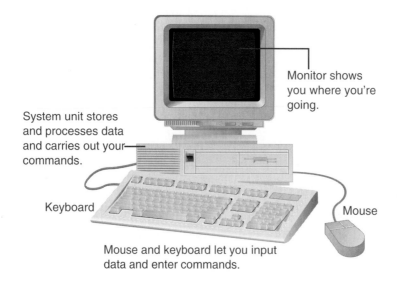

Monitor shows you where you're going.

System unit stores and processes data and carries out your commands.

Keyboard

Mouse

Mouse and keyboard let you input data and enter commands.

The System Unit

The system unit contains three basic elements: a *central processing unit* (CPU), which does all the "thinking" for the computer; *random-access memory* (RAM), which stores instructions and data while the CPU is processing them; and *disk drives,* which store information permanently on disks to keep the information safe. The system unit also contains several *ports* (at the back), which allow you to connect other devices to it, such as a keyboard, mouse, and printer.

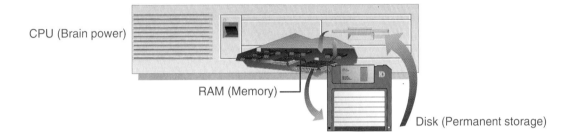

CPU (Brain power)

RAM (Memory)

Disk (Permanent storage)

Using a Mouse

Like the keyboard, a mouse allows you to communicate with the computer. You roll the mouse around on your desk to move a *mouse pointer* on the screen. You can use the pointer to open menus and select other items on-screen. Here are some mouse techniques you must master:

Pointing. To point, roll the mouse on your desk until the tip of the mouse pointer is on the item to which you want to point.

Clicking. To click on an item, point to the desired item, and then hold the mouse steady while you press and release the mouse button. Use the left mouse button unless I tell you specifically to use the right button.

Double-clicking. To double-click, hold the mouse steady while you press and release the mouse button twice quickly.

Right-clicking. To right-click, click using the right mouse button instead of the left button.

Drag. To drag, hold down the left mouse button and move the mouse to a new position.

Using a Keyboard

The keyboard is no mystery. It contains a set of *alphanumeric* (letter and number) keys for entering text, *arrow* keys for moving around on-screen, and *function* keys (F1, F2, and so on) for entering commands. It also has some odd keys, including *Alt* (Alternative), *Ctrl* (Control), and *Esc* (Escape) that perform special actions.

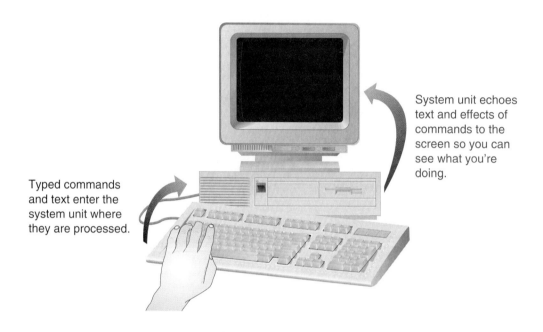

System unit echoes text and effects of commands to the screen so you can see what you're doing.

Typed commands and text enter the system unit where they are processed.

Understanding Disks, Directories, and Files

Whatever you type (a letter, a list of names, a tax return) is stored only in your computer's temporary memory, and is erased when the electricity is turned off. To protect your work, you must *save* it in a *file* on a *disk*.

A *file* is like a folder that you might use to store a report or a letter. You name the file, so you can later find and retrieve the information it contains.

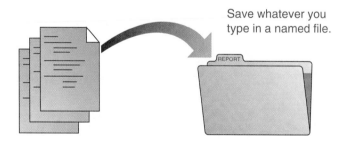

Save whatever you type in a named file.

REPORT

Files are stored on *disks*. Your computer probably has a *hard disk* inside it (called "drive C") to which you can save your files. You can also save files to *floppy disks*, which you insert into the slots (the floppy disk drives) on the front of the computer.

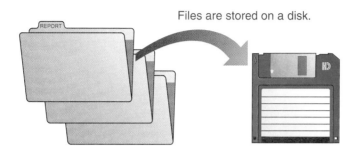

Files are stored on a disk.

To keep files organized on a disk, you can create *directories* on the disk. Each directory acts as a drawer in a filing cabinet, storing a group of related files. Although you can create directories on both floppy and hard disks, most people use directories only on hard disks.

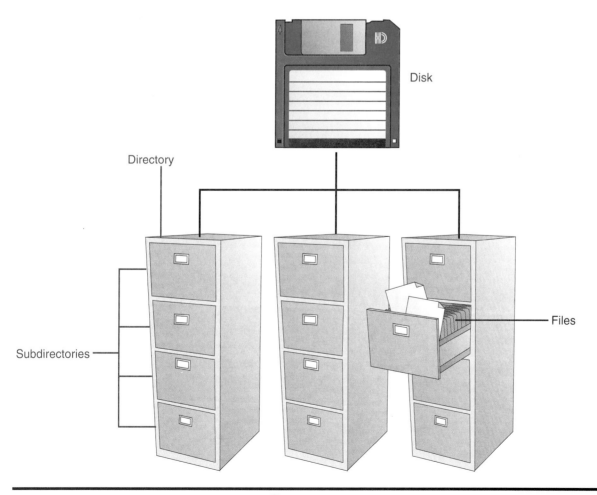

Disk

Directory

Subdirectories

Files

PART 1

Basic 1-2-3 for Windows Tasks

Before you can jump in and start swimming around your 1-2-3 for Windows program, you need to spend some time getting acquainted with the basics of the program—getting used to the water, so to speak. In this section, you will learn fundamentals, such as how to start the program, how to use the 1-2-3 menus and dialog boxes, and so on. These basic procedures will be the foundation of your 1-2-3 knowledge from which you will build on, so it's a good idea to master these procedures now.

- Starting Windows
- Starting 1-2-3
- Understanding the 1-2-3 Screen
- Using 1-2-3 Menus
- Working with 1-2-3 Dialog Boxes
- Working with SmartIcons
- Moving and Hiding SmartIcons
- Getting Help from 1-2-3
- Understanding the Worksheet Structure
- Moving Around the Worksheet Window
- Adding New Worksheets to a Worksheet File
- Navigating Between Worksheets
- Viewing Multiple Worksheets in a Worksheet File
- Exiting 1-2-3

STARTING WINDOWS

When to Start Windows

Before you can use 1-2-3, you must start Windows. Starting Windows will display the Windows desktop on your screen. You'll see the Program Manager, which you use to run other applications (such as 1-2-3).

If you've not yet installed the program, turn to the installation instructions at the back of this book for assistance.

Starting Windows

1 Turn on your computer and monitor.

2 At the DOS prompt, which looks like **C:>** or **C:\>**, type **win** and press **Enter**.

```
C:\>win  2
```

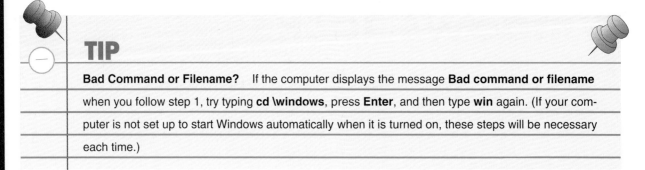

TIP

Bad Command or Filename? If the computer displays the message **Bad command or filename** when you follow step 1, try typing **cd \windows**, press **Enter**, and then type **win** again. (If your computer is not set up to start Windows automatically when it is turned on, these steps will be necessary each time.)

LEARNING THE LINGO

DOS prompt: A set of characters on the left side of the screen when you first turn on your computer, followed by a blinking underline. DOS commands are typed in at the DOS prompt.

Applications: Programs that run on your computer, such as spreadsheet, database, word processing, and graphics programs.

STARTING 1-2-3

When to Start 1-2-3

Once you have Windows up and running, you can then start 1-2-3. To start a program, use the Windows Program Manager screen, which is displayed when you first start Windows. You need to locate the Lotus Applications *icon*, a small graphical symbol with the label **Lotus Applications** below it. This icon represents the Lotus program group. Once opened, you'll see the Lotus Applications *program group window*. From the program group window, you can start 1-2-3.

The icons displayed on your Program Manager screen depend on the programs that are installed on your computer. Your screens will probably not look exactly the same as the ones shown in this book.

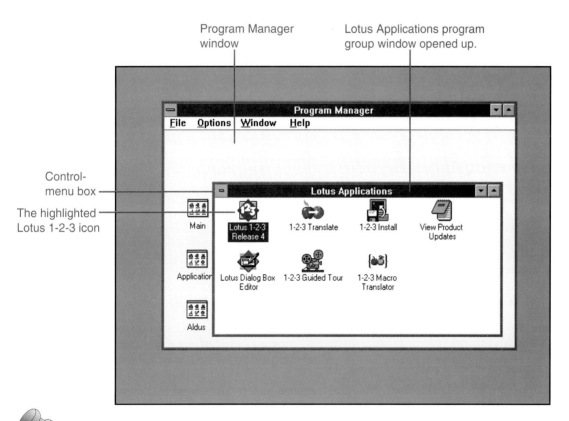

Program Manager window

Lotus Applications program group window opened up.

Control-menu box

The highlighted Lotus 1-2-3 icon

TIP

How Do You Open the Program Manager? If the Lotus Applications program group is not open, it appears at the bottom of the Program Manager window as an icon. You need to open the Program Group window in order to start 1-2-3 (as described in this task). To open it, double-click on the icon, or press **Ctrl+Tab** until the icon is highlighted. Then press **Enter** to open the program group.

Basic 1-2-3 for Windows Tasks

STARTING 1-2-3

Starting 1-2-3 for Windows

1 In the Windows Program Manager screen, move the mouse pointer directly over the **Lotus Applications** program group icon, and double-click on the left mouse button. If you're using the keyboard, press **Ctrl+Tab** until the icon is highlighted, and then press **Enter**.

2 When the Lotus Applications program group window is opened, move the mouse pointer directly over the **Lotus 1-2-3 Release 4** icon, and double-click on the left mouse button. If you're using the keyboard, press **Ctrl+Tab** until the icon is highlighted, and then press **Enter**.

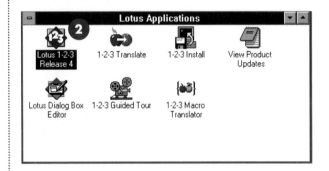

What's a Control-Menu Box?

The Control-menu box is an icon representing the Control menu. The Control menu is a menu common to all Windows programs. It's used to manipulate various Windows window features, such as closing, or resizing the window. You'll learn more about the Control menu in the task "Understanding the 1-2-3 Screen."

After you've exited the 1-2-3 program (explained in the "Exiting 1-2-3" task later in this section), you'll be returned to the Lotus Applications program group window. To close the window, double-click on the **Control-menu** box, or press **Ctrl+F4**.

LEARNING THE LINGO

Icon: A small picture on the screen that represents a program, an action you can take, or a piece of information.

Highlight: A solid color bar or outline around an icon or menu command that indicates you have selected it.

Worksheet: Work, such as a budget report or a balanced expense account, created using a spreadsheet program.

QUICK REFRESHER

As you learned in the Introduction, you can use the mouse to point and select items on-screen. Here are the mouse techniques you will need to use in this section:

Point: To move your mouse so that the arrow on-screen is directly over the item you want to select.

Click: A quick, light tap of the left mouse button while holding the mouse pointer steadily over the item to be selected.

Double-click: Two quick, light taps in a row on the left mouse button.

UNDERSTANDING THE 1-2-3 SCREEN

What Are the Parts of the 1-2-3 Screen?

When you first start 1-2-3, the opening title screen appears briefly, and then the following figure is displayed. It's a good idea to familiarize yourself with the parts of the screen and what each one does.

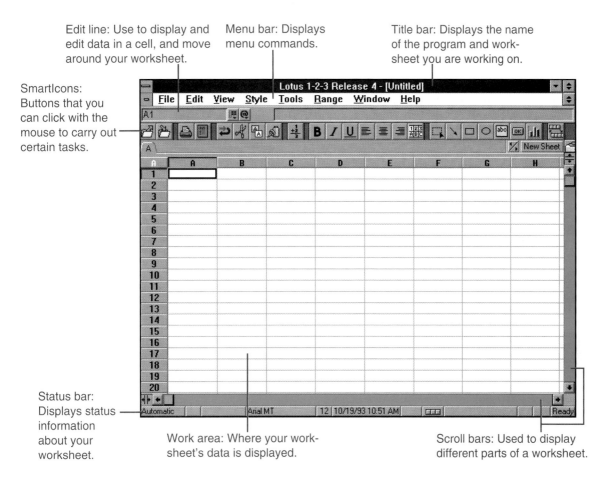

Edit line: Use to display and edit data in a cell, and move around your worksheet.

Menu bar: Displays menu commands.

Title bar: Displays the name of the program and worksheet you are working on.

SmartIcons: Buttons that you can click with the mouse to carry out certain tasks.

Status bar: Displays status information about your worksheet.

Work area: Where your worksheet's data is displayed.

Scroll bars: Used to display different parts of a worksheet.

LEARNING THE LINGO

Commands: Orders that tell the computer what to do.

Edit: Making changes to your data.

UNDERSTANDING THE 1-2-3 SCREEN

Are You a New Windows User?

If you're new to the world of Windows, there are a few basics that will help you with your program. Fortunately, these basics apply to all Windows programs, so if you learn them now, you can easily apply them to other Windows-based applications.

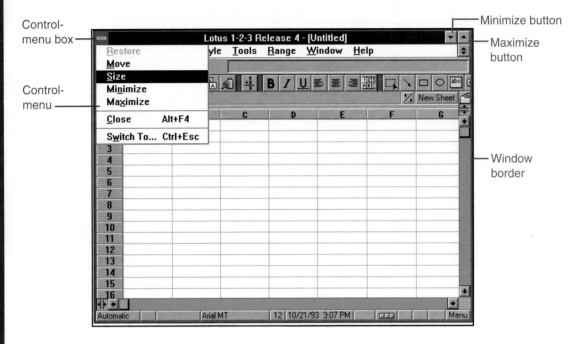

The Control-menu box, when activated, reveals a menu with commands for controlling the window itself, such as moving, sizing, and closing the window. To open the Control menu, click on the Control-menu box (shown in the figure above), or press Alt+Spacebar. Make your selection by clicking on the command name, or typing the selection letter (you'll learn more about menus in the task "Using 1-2-3 Menus").

Mouse users will find buttons to click to make the manipulating of the window faster. The Minimize and Maximize buttons are used to alter a window's size. The Minimize button shrinks the window into the size of an icon. The Maximize button enlarges the window to fill your screen. When the Maximize button shows a double-headed arrow, the Restore button, it will return the window to its original size.

To resize the window with the mouse, move the mouse pointer to a window border. When the pointer becomes a double-headed arrow, press the left mouse button and drag the border to a new position. To move a window, point to the title bar, press the left mouse button, and drag to a new location.

What Are Menus?

Menus are used to issue commands to 1-2-3, telling it what you want it to do. Menus offer lists of commands to choose from. You'll find the menu names displayed on the menu bar on your screen.

To use 1-2-3 menus and commands, you must first open the menu and then select a command. When you open a menu, it drops down to reveal a list of commands like those shown in the figure below. You can use the mouse or the keyboard to select menu commands. Notice that each menu name and command has an underlined letter. This is called the *selection letter*.

If you're using the keyboard to select a menu from the menu bar, you can hold down the **Alt** key and press the underlined selection letter to reveal the menu. When a menu list is revealed, you can choose commands from the list by typing the corresponding selection letter. If you're using the mouse, point to the menu name or the menu item you want to select, and click the left mouse button. When a menu command is highlighted, a brief description of the command appears in the title bar.

When you select a command from the menu bar, the corresponding menu is displayed.

Menu bar: Lists 1-2-3 menus.

A command description appears here when a menu command is highlighted.

Highlight bar: Indicates the command currently selected.

Menu commands displayed in light gray text are not available at the present time.

Selection letter: Underlined command letters that can be activated with the keyboard.

Shortcut keys: A combination of keys that can be pressed on the keyboard to activate a command without opening the menu.

Submenu arrow: Reveals another menu list to choose from when selected.

Ellipsis (...): Indicates that selecting the command will display a dialog box.

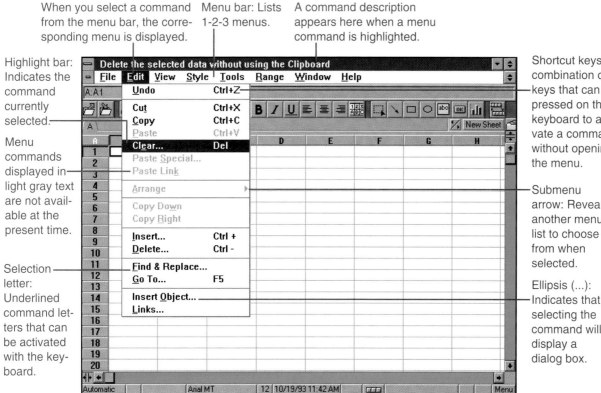

Basic 1-2-3 for Windows Tasks

USING 1-2-3 MENUS

Selecting Menu Commands

1 Click on the menu name on the menu bar. Or hold down the **Alt** key, and then type the underlined letter in the menu name.

2 Click on the command name, or type the underlined letter in the command name.

LEARNING THE LINGO

Shortcut key: A key, or combination of keys, you can use to issue a command without using the menus.

Ellipsis: Three dots (periods) following a menu command, which indicate that a dialog box will follow when selected.

Selection letter: The underlined letter of the command or menu name. Keyboard users can select a command by typing the selection letter or can select a menu by holding down **Alt** and typing the selection letter.

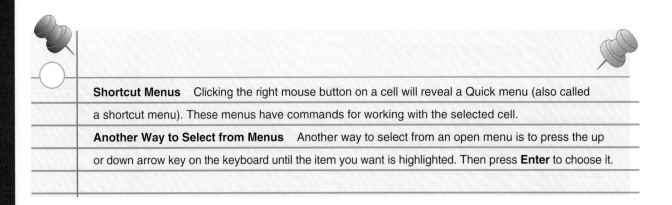

Shortcut Menus   Clicking the right mouse button on a cell will reveal a Quick menu (also called a shortcut menu). These menus have commands for working with the selected cell.

Another Way to Select from Menus   Another way to select from an open menu is to press the up or down arrow key on the keyboard until the item you want is highlighted. Then press **Enter** to choose it.

Exercise

Follow these steps to practice choosing menu commands.

1 Click on **View** or press **Alt+V**.

2 Click on **Z**oom In, or press **Z**.

3 Click on **View**, or press **Alt+V**.

4 Click on Zoom **O**ut, or press **O**.

5 Click on **Help**, or press **Alt+H**.

6 Click on **A**bout 1-2-3, or press **A**.

7 Click on **OK**, or press **Esc**.

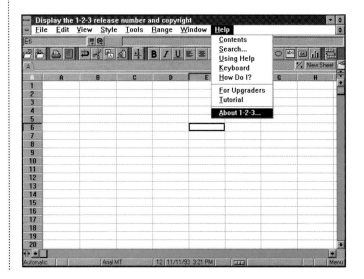

TIP

Oops! I've Changed My Mind! If you start to select a menu com-mand but then change your mind, press **Esc**.

Basic 1-2-3 for Windows Tasks

WORKING WITH DIALOG BOXES

What Is a Dialog Box?

1-2-3 displays a *dialog box* when it needs more information from you before it can carry out a task. A dialog box is simply a window with options or more details that help you with your work. A dialog box may appear when you enter a menu command or select certain command buttons. Even though every dialog box is different, they all share many common elements. If you learn how to use these elements, you'll be able to use any dialog box you encounter.

You can use your mouse to click on the different parts of the dialog box. Or you can use the keyboard by pressing the **Tab** key to highlight options or pressing **Alt** and choosing selection letters. Once all the settings in the dialog box are the way you want them, you can exit the box to carry out the command or task.

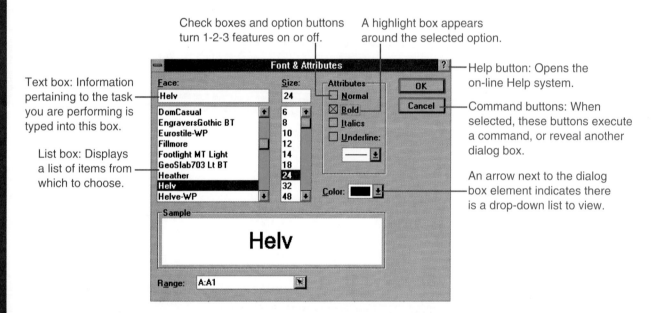

Check boxes and option buttons turn 1-2-3 features on or off.

A highlight box appears around the selected option.

Text box: Information pertaining to the task you are performing is typed into this box.

List box: Displays a list of items from which to choose.

Help button: Opens the on-line Help system.

Command buttons: When selected, these buttons execute a command, or reveal another dialog box.

An arrow next to the dialog box element indicates there is a drop-down list to view.

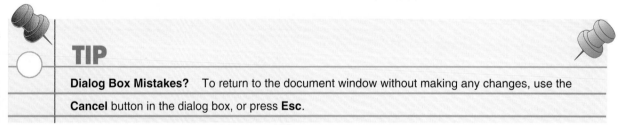

TIP

Dialog Box Mistakes?   To return to the document window without making any changes, use the **Cancel** button in the dialog box, or press **Esc**.

How to Use a Dialog Box

To choose any item in a dialog box, click on it, or press **Alt** plus the item's selection letter. Keyboard users can also press the **Tab** key to move from option to option. Once the item is selected, use the item as noted in this table:

Text box. Click or use the left and right arrow keys to position the cursor and type an entry. If you make a mistake, use **Del** and **Backspace** to correct.

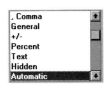

List box. Double-click on the item you want, or use the arrow keys to highlight the item. If the box has scroll bars, click on the scroll arrows to see portions of the list, or use the keyboard arrow keys to scroll.

Drop-down list. Click on the down arrow to display the list, or press **Alt** plus the selection letter. Press **Alt+↓** to see all the options. You can also use the down arrow or the **Spacebar** on the keyboard. Click on the item you want, or highlight the item with the arrow keys.

Combo box. Enter text in the box as you would in a text box, or click the desired item in the list. If you're using the keyboard, tab to the list box, and use the arrow keys to highlight an item. Once highlighted, the list item will appear in the text box.

Number box. Type a number in the box, or click the up and down arrows to increase or decrease the value.

Check box. Click on the box to turn it on or off. If you're using the keyboard, press **Alt+** the selection letter.

Option button. Click on a button to turn it on and turn all others in the group off. You can also use the arrow keys on the keyboard. You can only select one option button in a group of related options.

Command button. Click the button to execute or cancel the dialog box selections. Keyboard users can press **Alt** and the selection letters, or tab to the button and press **Enter**.

Help button. Click this button, or press **F1**, to get help with the particular dialog box you're working with.

Basic 1-2-3 for Windows Tasks

WORKING WITH SMARTICONS

What Is a SmartIcon?

SmartIcons are small graphic symbols that look like buttons on the 1-2-3 screen. Each one performs a particular task or command. SmartIcons are shortcuts to using menu commands and sequences. Rather than pull down a menu and then select a command, you can just click on a SmartIcon button instead. You'll soon find that selecting a button can be a lot faster than working with menus.

To select a SmartIcon button, use the mouse pointer to point and click on the desired button. (Sorry, you can't use the keyboard to select SmartIcons.) Some buttons will execute a command right away, such as **Paste**. Other buttons, such as the **Save** button, will open a dialog box.

	Opens an existing worksheet file.		Aligns data to the left.
	Saves the current worksheet.		Centers data.
	Prints the worksheet.		Aligns data to the right.
	Previews the worksheet page.		Completes a sequence in a selected range.
	Undoes the last action.		Select several objects.
	Cuts selected data to the Clipboard.		Draws an arrow.
	Copies selected data to the Clipboard.		Draws a square or rectangle.
	Pastes data from the Clipboard.		Draws a circle or ellipse.
	Sums values above or to the left.		Draws a text box.
	Bolds data.		Draws a macro button.
	Italicizes data.		Creates a new graph from the selected range.
	Underlines data.		Displays the next set of SmartIcons.

More SmartIcons!

Depending upon the task you are performing, 1-2-3 displays different SmartIcon sets. For example, there will be one set of SmartIcons available when you're entering data, and another set available when you're drawing a graph. The default SmartIcon set, the set that appears when you first start 1-2-3, contains the most frequently used buttons. You can also customize your SmartIcons for your own usage as well.

To find out what kind of command or task a SmartIcon button repre-sents, point to the button, and then press and hold the right mouse button. A brief description of the command or task appears in the title bar. You'll learn more about using SmartIcons as you more tasks, but it's a good idea to familiarize yourself with what they look like now so you'll be able to use them later.

Displaying Different SmartIcons Sets

There are eight different sets of 1-2-3 SmartIcons. You can display a different set by clicking on the SmartIcons button on the status bar.

List of
SmartIcon sets

Default Sheet
Editing
Formatting
Goodies
Macro Building
Printing
Sheet Auditing
WorkingTogether
Hide SmartIcons

A list of SmartIcons sets appears. Select the set you want from the list. The new buttons will be displayed.

LEARNING THE LINGO

Clipboard: A temporary storage area for text and graphics.

Basic 1-2-3 for Windows Tasks

MOVING AND HIDING SMARTICONS

Why Move or Hide the SmartIcons?

Some occasions may arise where you would like more room on your screen to work with your data, or perhaps you would like the SmartIcons positioned differently for your convenience. To solve these types of problems, 1-2-3 lets you move the SmartIcons to different locations on the screen or hide them all together.

You can easily change the positions of the SmartIcons, such as placing them on the left, right, top, or bottom of the screen. You can also let them float in the middle of your worksheet in their own little mobile window. The figure below shows a floating set of SmartIcons.

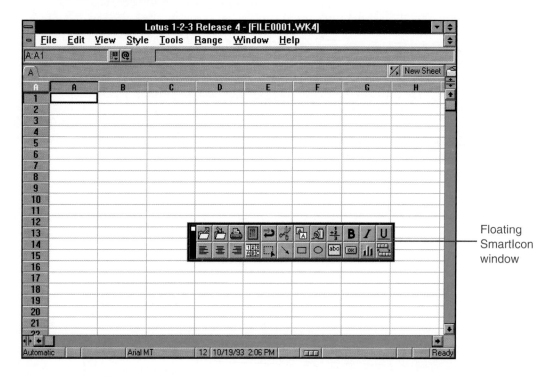

Floating
SmartIcon
window

Moving SmartIcons

1 Click on Tools, or press **Alt+T**.

2 Click on SmartIcons, or press **I**.

3 When the SmartIcons dialog box appears, select the desired position for the button palette from the **P**osition drop-down box.

4 Select **OK**, or press **Enter** to exit the dialog box and move the SmartIcons.

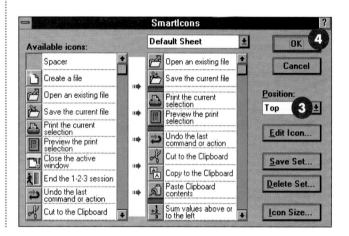

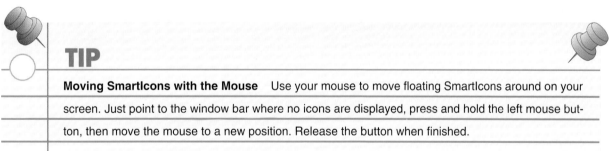

TIP

Moving SmartIcons with the Mouse   Use your mouse to move floating SmartIcons around on your screen. Just point to the window bar where no icons are displayed, press and hold the left mouse button, then move the mouse to a new position. Release the button when finished.

Basic 1-2-3 for Windows Tasks

MOVING AND HIDING SMARTICONS

Hiding or Displaying SmartIcons

1 Click on **View**, or press **Alt+V**.

2 Click on Set View **Preferences**, or press **P**.

3 In the Show in 1-2-3 section of the dialog box, click on SmartIcons, or press **Alt+I** to turn the checkbox off. An **X** in the check box means the SmartIcons are revealed, no X means they are hidden. (To display the SmartIcons again, repeat these steps, and place an **X** in the check box.)

4 Select **OK**, or press **Enter**.

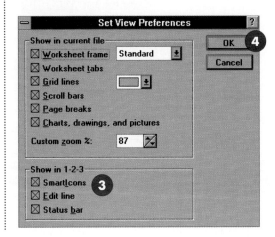

GETTING HELP FROM 1-2-3

What Is Help?

Help is on-screen assistance from the 1-2-3 for Windows program for any problems you encounter. For example, if you are saving a document and an unfamiliar dialog box appears on your screen, you could access the on-line Help feature to find out what to do. 1-2-3 has a sophisticated Help system that can display information on-screen about any 1-2-3 task.

1-2-3's Help facility has several unique features that assist you in finding the information you need. You'll find many of them on the **H**elp menu, including a Table of Contents and specific instructions about using Help. The Help system is also *context-sensitive*, meaning that you can get help when you're in the middle of a task. 1-2-3 knows what point in the program you are seeking help for. It will take you directly to the Help section that explains all about the task you are trying to perform.

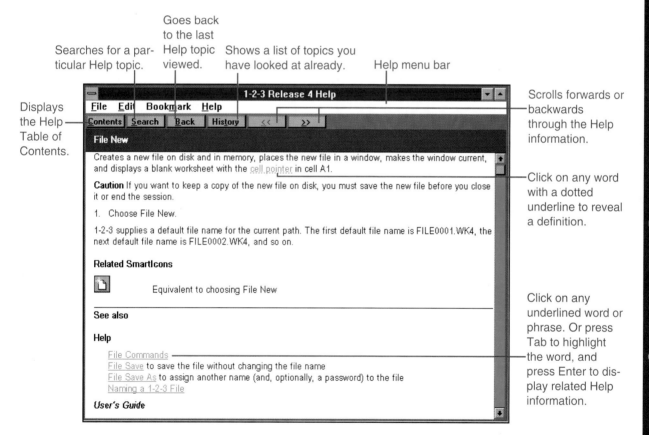

Searches for a particular Help topic.

Goes back to the last Help topic viewed.

Shows a list of topics you have looked at already.

Help menu bar

Displays the Help Table of Contents.

Scrolls forwards or backwards through the Help information.

Click on any word with a dotted underline to reveal a definition.

Click on any underlined word or phrase. Or press Tab to highlight the word, and press Enter to display related Help information.

LEARNING THE LINGO

Context-sensitive: A Help system that takes you directly to the information pertaining to the task you are trying to perform, without routing you through a topical index.

GETTING HELP FROM 1-2-3

Using Help

1 Click on **Help**, or press **Alt+H**.

2 Press **C**, or click on Contents.

3 Click on an underlined topic to view related information.

4 Click on the Contents button, or press **C** at any time to return to the Help Contents screen.

5 Double-click on the **Control-menu** box, or press **Alt+4** to close Help.

TIP

Fast Help   Press **F1** while any dialog box is displayed, or click on the tiny question mark icon in the upper right corner of the box to see Help information about that dialog box.

UNDERSTANDING THE WORKSHEET STRUCTURE

What Is a Worksheet?

Worksheets organize the data you enter. Worksheets are comprised of columns and rows that intersect to form boxes, called *cells*. Worksheets are rather like large grid pages upon which you can total numbers in columns and rows, perform calculations on designated values, and execute complex mathematical formulas.

A worksheet page in 1-2-3 is ruled into 8,192 rows and 256 columns. Columns are labeled with alphabet letters, such as A through Z, AA through ZZ, BA through BZ, and so on through IV. Rows are labeled with numbers, 1 through 8,192.

Each cell in a worksheet has a unique name, or address designating its location. For example, the top left cell in every worksheet is named A1. That's where column A intersects with row 1. Cell names, also called *references*, always refer to the column first, and then the row.

The cell reference is diaplsyed in the Edit line.

Row —

Column

Cell B5

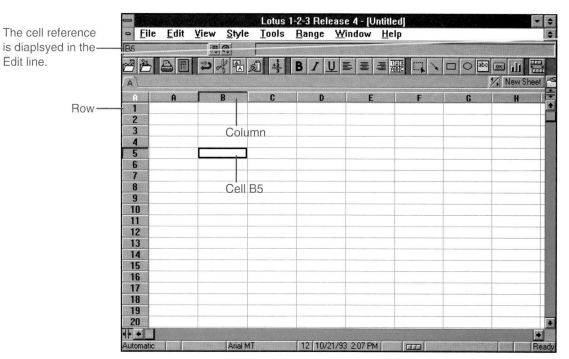

TIP

More! 1-2-3 for Windows can contain up to 256 worksheets per file, rather like a 256-page book.

Each new file starts with a single worksheet, however, you can add up to 255 more if you need to!

See the task "Adding New Worksheets to a Worksheet File" to learn how.

MOVING AROUND THE WORKSHEET WINDOW

Why Move Around the Worksheet?

As you learned in the previous task, worksheets can cover a lot of area with numerous rows and columns. You'll need to learn how to move around your worksheet in order to enter, edit, and view your data.

You can use the mouse or the keyboard to move around the worksheet. If you're using the mouse, click on any cell to make it active. An *active cell* is surrounded by a dark outline called a *cell pointer* (also known as a *highlight* box, or *selector*). If you're using the keyboard, you can highlight different cells by pressing the keyboard arrow keys. You can also move along the worksheet in greater increments with the scroll bars.

An active cell is highlighted with a darker box.

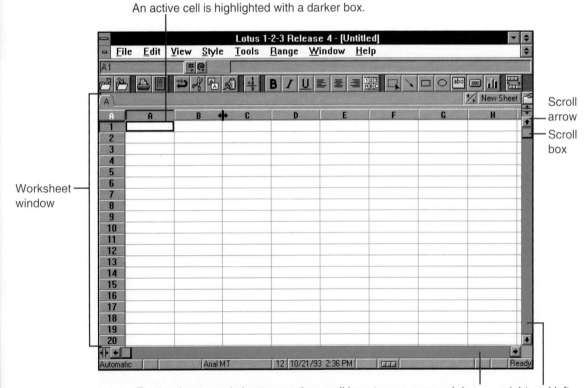

Worksheet window

Scroll arrow

Scroll box

To view larger worksheets, use the scroll bars to move up and down, or right and left.

LEARNING THE LINGO

Active cell: A cell that is currently highlighted with a darker border or box (called a cell pointer or selector) that is ready for data to be entered.

30

Moving Around with the Mouse

You can move around the worksheet window with the mouse by clicking or dragging on the vertical or horizontal scroll bars.

Scroll Bar Movements

To Scroll   Do This

To Scroll	Do This
Up or down one row	Click the up or down arrow on the vertical scroll bar.
Left or right one column	Click the left or right arrow on the horizontal scroll bar.
Up or down one screen	Click between the up or down arrow and the scroll box on the vertical scroll bar.
Left or right one screen	Click between the left or right arrow and the scroll box on the horizontal scroll bar.
To the top or bottom row	Drag the scroll box to the top or bottom of the vertical scroll bar.
To the leftmost or rightmost column	Drag the scroll box to the left or right end of the horizontal scroll bar.

TIP

My Mouse Keeps Changing!   When moving the mouse pointer around the worksheet window, you'll notice it sometimes changes appearance, depending on where it's located on the screen. When your mouse pointer crosses a column or row border, it becomes a double-headed arrow. You can then click and drag the border to make a larger or smaller row or column. When your mouse pointer moves over a selected cell, it becomes a hand icon, which you can use to move data from that cell to another.

Basic 1-2-3 for Windows Tasks

MOVING AROUND THE WORKSHEET WINDOW

Moving Around with the Keyboard

You can move around the worksheet window with the keyboard by pressing the *cursor movement keys* (such as the arrow keys or *combination keys*), for example, **Ctrl+Home**.

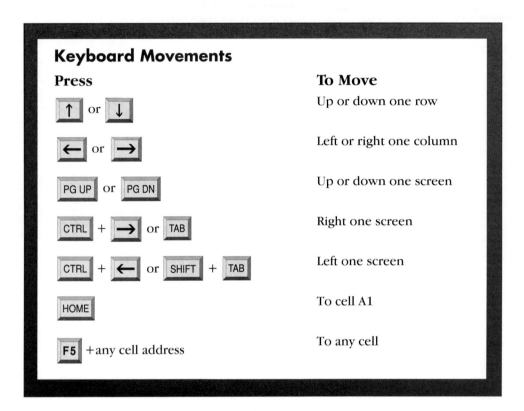

Keyboard Movements

Press	To Move
↑ or ↓	Up or down one row
← or →	Left or right one column
PG UP or PG DN	Up or down one screen
CTRL + → or TAB	Right one screen
CTRL + ← or SHIFT + TAB	Left one screen
HOME	To cell A1
F5 +any cell address	To any cell

QUICK REFRESHER

Here are the mouse techniques you need to master as you move around the document window:

Point: To move your mouse so that the arrow on-screen is directly over the item you want to select.

Click: A quick, light tap of the left mouse button while holding the mouse pointer steadily over the item to be selected.

Double-click: On the left mouse button, two quick, light taps in a row.

Drag: To press the mouse button and move the mouse to a new position before releasing the button.

ADDING NEW WORKSHEETS TO A WORKSHEET FILE

When Do You Add Worksheets?

When you start 1-2-3, a single worksheet appears in the worksheet window, worksheet A. Worksheets are identified by labeled tabs, as shown in the figure below. Most of the time, a single worksheet is all that you will need. However, some spreadsheet projects you create may require more than one worksheet. In these cases, simply add an additional worksheet to your worksheet file. This will add another labeled tab in the worksheet window.

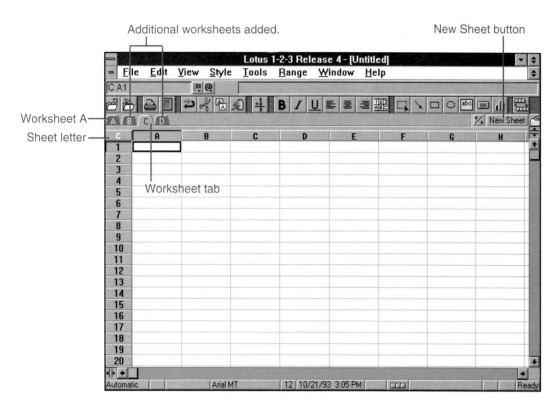

Additional worksheets added.

New Sheet button

Worksheet A

Sheet letter

Worksheet tab

![TIP pushpin]

TIP

New Worksheet Shortcut To quickly insert a single new worksheet, click the **New Sheet** button located in your worksheet window. This will automatically add a worksheet behind your current worksheet, and bring it to the front of the window.

New Sheet

In the Insert dialog box, use the **Q**uantity option to add more than one new worksheet at a time.

ADDING NEW WORKSHEETS TO A WORKSHEET FILE

Adding a New Worksheet

1 Click on Edit, or press **Alt+E**.

2 Click on Insert, or press **I**.

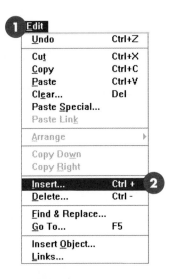

3 When the Insert dialog box appears, click on the Sheet option button, or press **S**.

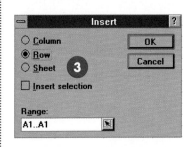

4 Click on **Before**, or press **B**, to insert a new worksheet before the current sheet. Click on After, or press **F**, to insert a new worksheet after the current sheet.

5 Click on **OK**, or press **Enter**.

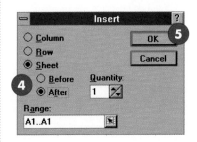

ADDING NEW WORKSHEETS TO A WORKSHEET FILE

More About Worksheets

By default, 1-2-3 labels your worksheets with alphabetical names, worksheet A, B, and so on. You can rename your worksheet tabs. Just double-click on the tab and type a new name, up to 15 characters long. When finished, press Enter. To delete a name, double-click on the tab, press Del and Enter.

To delete a worksheet, Click on the tab of the sheet you want to delete to bring it to the front of the window. Click on the sheet letter to select the entire worksheet. Click the right mouse button to reveal a Quick menu, and select Delete, or press Ctrl+− (the minus sign on the numeric keypad).

If your worksheet file contains more than one worksheet, all it takes is a click of the mouse to move to the next sheet. Clicking on a worksheet tab will quickly bring the worksheet to the front of the worksheet window.

Basic 1-2-3 for Windows Tasks

VIEWING MULTIPLE WORKSHEETS IN A WORKSHEET FILE

Why View Multiple Worksheets?

When you're working with more than one worksheet in your file, it's often convenient to be able to see several on your screen at the same time. 1-2-3 for Windows allows you to view three worksheets in the worksheet window area.

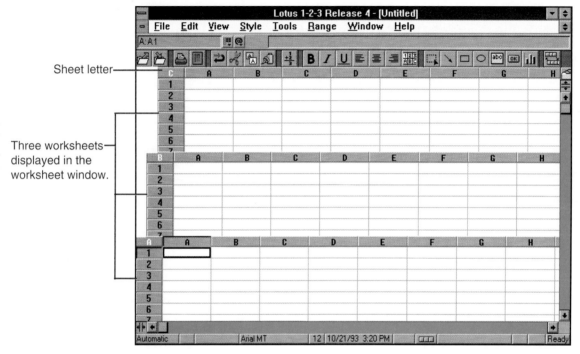

Sheet letter

Three worksheets displayed in the worksheet window.

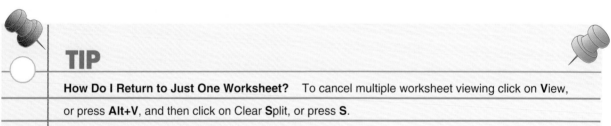

TIP

How Do I Return to Just One Worksheet? To cancel multiple worksheet viewing click on **V**iew, or press **Alt+V**, and then click on Clear **S**plit, or press **S**.

Viewing Multiple Worksheets at Once

1 Click on View, or press Alt+V.

2 Click on Split, or press **S**.

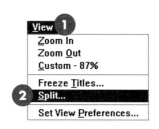

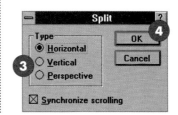

3 When the Split dialog box appears, click on **P**erspective or press **P**.

4 Click on **OK**, or press **Enter**.

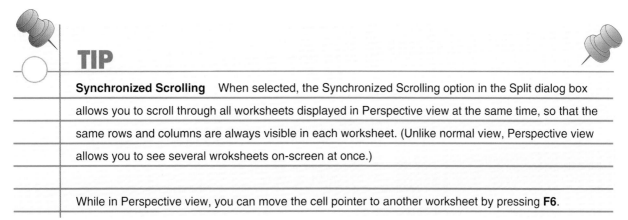

TIP

Synchronized Scrolling When selected, the Synchronized Scrolling option in the Split dialog box allows you to scroll through all worksheets displayed in Perspective view at the same time, so that the same rows and columns are always visible in each worksheet. (Unlike normal view, Perspective view allows you to see several wroksheets on-screen at once.)

While in Perspective view, you can move the cell pointer to another worksheet by pressing **F6**.

Basic 1-2-3 for Windows Tasks

EXITING 1-2-3

When Do You Exit 1-2-3?

When you're finished working in 1-2-3, you should exit the program. This frees up the system resources that 1-2-3 is using so that you can run a different program. (See the "Closing a Worksheet" task for further information on exiting 1-2-3.)

You should always exit 1-2-3 before you turn off your computer. This ensures that all the 1-2-3 worksheets you have created are saved onto disk, so that you can retrieve them later.

Exiting 1-2-3

1 Click on File or press **Alt+F**.

2 Click on Exit or press **X**.

Save Changes to Document?

If you're trying to exit the program without saving your current document, a dialog box will appear, asking you whether you want to save your changes. Click on (or tab to) the Cancel button, and you'll return to the document window. Click on No or press N, and you'll exit without saving. Click on Yes or press Y, and the Save As dialog box will appear for you to name and save your file. (See the "Saving a Document" task in Part 2.)

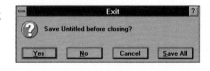

TIP

Fast Getaway   If you're using the mouse, you can exit the program quickly by pointing at the program's Control-menu box and double-clicking. If you're using the keyboard, press **Alt+F4**.

PART 2

Creating and Saving Worksheets

In this part, you will learn the skills necessary for creating worksheets, performing calculations, and saving all of your work. You'll also learn about ranges, formulas, and built-in functions.

- Entering Data

- Selecting Ranges

- Naming Ranges

- Entering Formulas

- Using Operators and Operator Precedence

- Understanding Relative and Absolute Cell Referencing

- Using Built-In Functions

- Saving a Worksheet

ENTERING DATA

What Is Data?

Data is information that you type into a 1-2-3 worksheet. Data can be a *value*, a *label*, or a *formula* (you'll learn more about formulas in the "Writing Formulas" task). Numbers are values, because they can be calculated and placed into formulas. All other characters, such as text, are considered labels, because they cannot be used for calculations. Knowing that, 1-2-3 can tell whether your data is a value or a label based on the characters you type in. For instance, typing in the letter **A** automatically causes 1-2-3 to treat the data as a label. Typing in the number **7** causes 1-2-3 to treat the data as a value.

When you start typing an entry into a worksheet cell, the characters you type appear in the cell and also in the *Contents box* located on the Edit line. The Edit line has several useful buttons for entering data. Click on the **Confirm** button to okay an entry after you've typed it. Click on the **Cancel** button to cancel your entry.

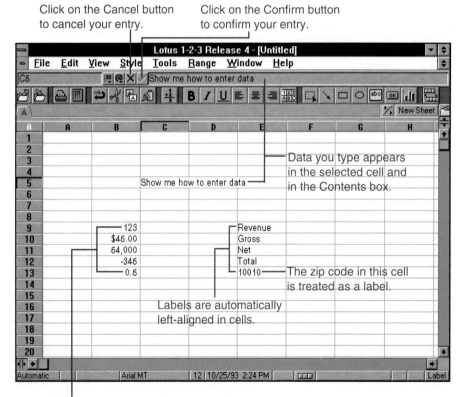

Click on the Cancel button to cancel your entry.

Click on the Confirm button to confirm your entry.

Data you type appears in the selected cell and in the Contents box.

The zip code in this cell is treated as a label.

Labels are automatically left-aligned in cells.

Values are automatically right-aligned in cells.

40

Entering Values

1 Click on the cell where you want to enter a value, or use the keyboard arrow keys to move the cell pointer to the desired cell.

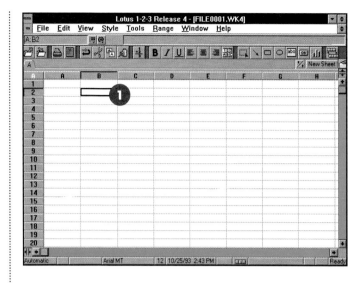

2 Type in the value.

3 To confirm the entry, click on another cell or click on the **Confirm** box in the Edit line. If you're using the keyboard, press **Enter** or an arrow key to confirm.

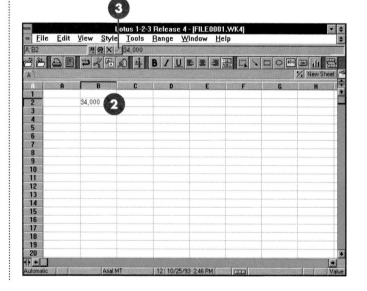

TIP

Oops! If you make a mistake while entering your data, simply use the **Backspace** key to back up, and retype your entry.

Creating and Saving Worksheets

ENTERING DATA

Entering Labels

1 Click on the cell where you want to enter a label, or use the keyboard arrow keys to move the cell pointer to the desired cell.

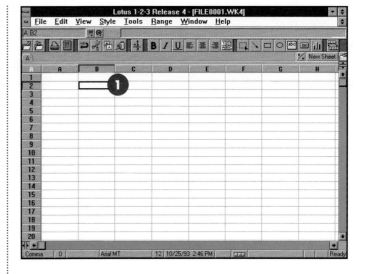

2 Type in the label. Be sure to include a label-prefix character, if necessary.

3 To confirm the entry, click on another cell, or click on the **Confirm** box in the Edit line. If you're using the keyboard, press **Enter** to confirm.

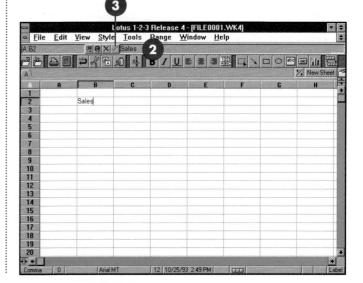

What's a Value?

A value is a number, but it's also any of these characters, which are used in calculating:

- $\quad+-.\;($

- Any currency symbol, such as $

By default, value entries are automatically right-aligned in the cell.

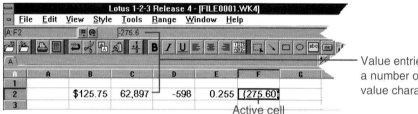

Value entries must start with a number or a designated value character.

Active cell

Entering Dates and Times

Dates and times are stored as special numbers, called date serial numbers, in 1-2-3 for Windows. Serial date numbers are based on the number of days between January 1, 1900 and the current date. For example, December 31, 2099 would be stored by 1-2-3 as the number 73050.

Enter a date or time in one of these formats:

Date or Time	Type
Day-month-year	20-Jun-94
Day-month	20-Jun
Long international	6/20/94
Long AM/PM	10:30:45 PM
Short AM/PM	10:30 PM
Long 24-hour	22:30:15
Short 24-hour	22:30

1-2-3 recognizes your entry as a date or time if you use one of these formats, and automatically converts the entry into a date serial number representing the date or time. You won't actually see the serial number in your cell, but 1-2-3 reads it as a serial number.

43

ENTERING DATA

What's a Label?

A label is a sequence of characters that cannot be used for calculations, such as a person's name or a place. Labels are automatically left-aligned, which is a good way to tell at a glance whether an entry is a label or a value (values are right-aligned by default).

However, sometimes you need to use numbers, such as zip codes—which 1-2-3 considers values—as labels rather than values. How do you tell 1-2-3 that your number entry is a label and not a value?

Label-prefix characters let you designate numbers as labels:

- ' for left alignment
- " for right alignment
- ^ for center alignment

Type in one of these label-prefix characters before you type your data to designate your entry as a label. The prefix does not show up in your cell, it's merely used as a code.

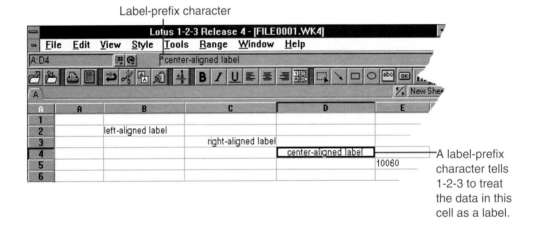

Label-prefix character

A label-prefix character tells 1-2-3 to treat the data in this cell as a label.

ENTERING DATA

Exercise

Practice entering data by following these steps:

1 Select a cell in an empty work-sheet.

2 Type **123**, and click on the **Confirm** box, or press **Enter**. 1-2-3 treats this data as a value and right-aligns it in the cell.

3 Select another cell in the work-sheet.

4 Type **Show Me**, and click on the **Confirm** box, or press **Enter**. 1-2-3 treats this data as a label and left-aligns it in the cell.

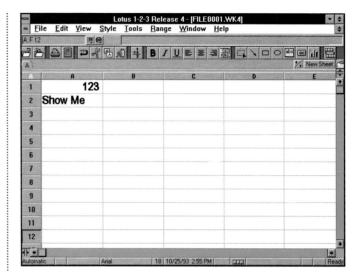

LEARNING THE LINGO

Data: Information that is entered into your worksheet: values, labels, formulas. Data includes text, numbers, and mathematical calculations.

Value: A number that can be used for calculations in a worksheet.

Label: Text or other data that cannot be used for calculations in a worksheet.

Formula: An instruction that tells 1-2-3 to combine or manipulate values in mathematical calculations. Formulas range in complexity and purpose.

Creating and Saving Worksheets

SELECTING RANGES

What Is a Range?

With many of your worksheet projects, you will want certain 1-2-3 commands to affect more than one cell at a time. For example, you may want all of the cells in rows B through D to have bold type. Or perhaps you would like five cells in column F to perform a certain calculation. Rather than click on each cell individually and apply the commands, you can select a range of cells to affect.

A *range* is a rectangular group of cells that is defined by its upper left corner and its lower right corner, and its worksheet letter, if necessary. **A3..D8** is a single worksheet range containing cells A3, B3, C3, and so on up to cell D8. An ellipsis (..) means "through." **B:C3..B:E10** is a range in worksheet B containing cells C3, D3, E3, and so on up to cell E10. A range can be as small as a single cell, or as large as an entire worksheet. You can use ranges to erase data, copy, move, or apply a variety of formatting and formula commands.

Click on the sheet label box to select the whole worksheet as a range.

The cell reference area shows the address of the selected range.

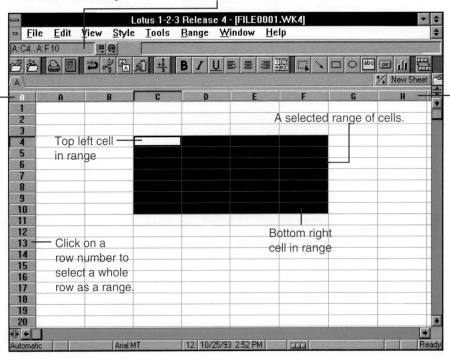

Click on a column letter to select a whole column as a range.

A selected range of cells.

Top left cell in range

Bottom right cell in range

Click on a row number to select a whole row as a range.

Selecting a Range

1 Move the cell pointer to the upper left corner of the range you want to select.

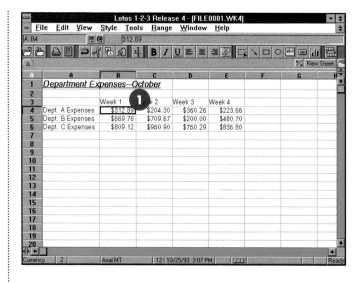

2 Press and hold the left mouse button, and drag the mouse pointer to the lower right corner of the range you want to select, and then release the mouse button. The selected range is highlighted. Or with the keyboard, press **F4**, and use the arrow keys to move to the lower right corner of your range. Then press **Enter** to select.

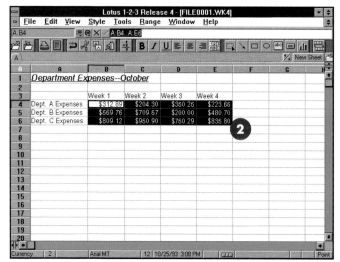

Select all of the cells in a column or row by clicking on the column or row heading. To highlight several columns or rows for a range, hold down the Ctrl key while you click on the column or row headings. To select an entire worksheet as a range, click on the sheet label box (the box in the upper left corner of the worksheet window).

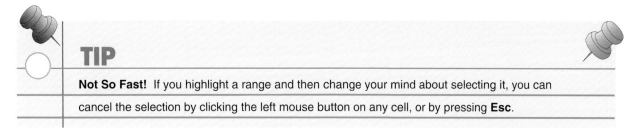

TIP

Not So Fast! If you highlight a range and then change your mind about selecting it, you can

cancel the selection by clicking the left mouse button on any cell, or by pressing **Esc**.

Creating and Saving Worksheets

SELECTING RANGES

3-D Ranges

If you're working with several worksheets at the same time, you can select a range that spans two or more worksheets in a worksheet file. A 3-D range contains the same columns and rows in each worksheet.

1 Move the mouse pointer to the first worksheet where the range will be included, and select the first cell in the range.

2 Press the left mouse button, and drag the mouse to highlight the range. If you're using the keyboard, press F4, and use the arrow keys to highlight the range. Then press Enter.

3 Press and hold the Shift key, and click the tab of the last worksheet to also use the same range. If you're using the keyboard, hold down the Shift key, press Ctrl+PgUp or Ctrl+PgDn to include the range in other worksheets, and then press Enter.

Exercise

Type in the text shown, and follow these steps to practice selecting a range:

1 Move the pointer to cell A2.

2 Drag the mouse pointer to cell B4, or press **F4** and use the keyboard arrow keys.

3 Release the mouse button, or press **Enter**. Range **A2..B4** is selected.

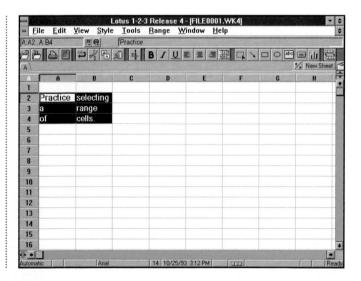

LEARNING THE LINGO

Range: A rectangular group of cells that is defined by its upper left and lower right corners, and worksheet letter.

NAMING RANGES

Why Name a Range?

By default, 1-2-3 names a range by its *address*—where it's located, such as C4..E7. But if you plan on using a range over and over again, it's a good idea to give it a name that easily signifies what it is or how you plan on using it. For example, perhaps you've assigned the name SALES94 to range A5..D7. Whenever you want to refer to that range or use it in a calculation, you can use the name SALES94 instead of remembering the actual range address. Range names are saved with the worksheet file.

The reference area shows the selected range address.

Click here to see a drop-down list of existing range names.

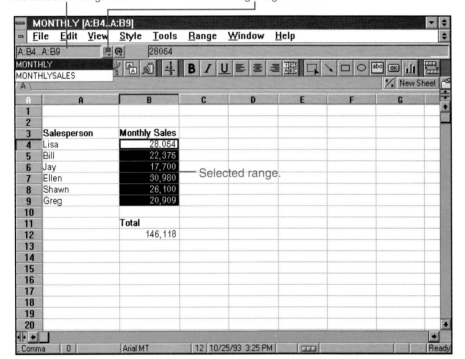

Selected range.

TIP

Quick Menu Shortcut A faster way to display the Name dialog box is to highlight the range, and click inside the range with the right mouse button. A Quick menu appears. Select **Name...** from the menu list, and the Name dialog box appears.

Creating and Saving Worksheets

NAMING RANGES

Naming a Range

1 Select the range to be named.

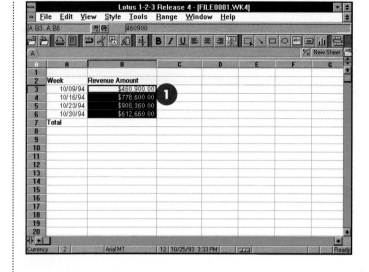

2 Click on the **R**ange menu, or press **Alt+R**.

3 Click on **N**ame, or press **N**.

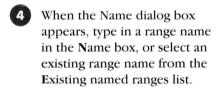

4 When the Name dialog box appears, type in a range name in the **N**ame box, or select an existing range name from the **E**xisting named ranges list.

5 Click on **OK**, or press **Enter**.

More on Naming Ranges

You can delete existing range names using the Name dialog box. Click on the existing range name in the Existing named ranges list, or type the name in the Name box. Click on the Delete button, or press Alt+D to delete the name. Use the Delete All button to erase all of the existing range names for that worksheet file.

A range name can be a word or phrase up to 15 characters long. However, there are quite a few characters that cannot be used in the name:

,	;
.	?
(space)	+
-	*
/	&
<	>
@	#
{	

Also avoid using names that look like cell addresses, use numbers, or @function (at function) names. (You'll learn about 1-2-3 @functions later.)

ENTERING FORMULAS

What's a Formula?

Formulas are one of 1-2-3's best features. A *formula* is a mathematical equation that performs a calculation on the values you've entered into your worksheet. For example, the formula +D7/12 calculates the result of dividing the contents of cell D7 by 12. You can use formulas to sum up groups of values, calculate averages, and perform financial analyses. Whenever you change your worksheet's data, existing formulas recalculate automatically for you, which keeps your worksheet up-to-date.

Formulas are entered like any other value or label. Select the cell to contain the formula, and then type in the formula. All formulas must begin with a number, a left parenthesis, a plus or minus sign, or the name of an @function. (You can learn more about 1-2-3's built-in formulas in the "Using Built-In Functions" task.) Unlike other data, once a formula is entered, only the result of the formula is displayed in the cell, but the formula is visible in the Contents box on the Edit line. Turn to the next task, "Using Operators and Operator Precedence" to learn how to write a formula.

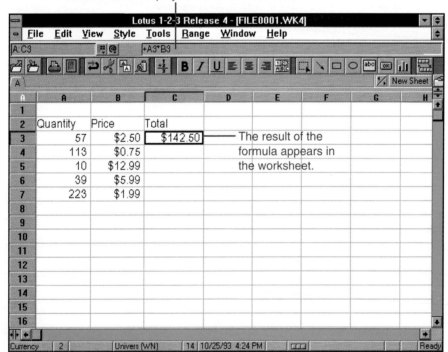

The formula is displayed in the Contents box.

The result of the formula appears in the worksheet.

52

Entering a Formula

1 Select the cell or cells in which you want a formula to perform a calculation.

2 Type in the formula.

3 Click on the **Confirm** box, or press **Enter**.

TIP

What's an ERR? When the letters **ERR** appear in your cell, 1-2-3 is telling you that it cannot evaluate the formula you entered. Check the formula for errors.

Creating and Saving Worksheets

ENTERING FORMULAS

Exercise

Follow these steps to practice entering a formula.

1 Select cell A1, type in a value, and click on the **Confirm** button, or press **Enter**.

2 Select cell B1, type in a value, and click on the **Confirm** button, or press **Enter**.

3 Select cell C1, type in the formula **+A1+B1**, and click the **Confirm** button, or press **Enter**.

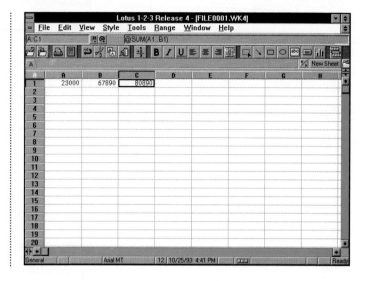

Sample Formulas

Here are a few examples of 1-2-3 formulas:

If you type:	The cell displays:
+C3	The contents of cell C3.
+D7+D8+D9	The sum of the values in cells D7, D8, and D9.
50/5	**10** (50 divided by 5).

USING OPERATORS AND OPERATOR PRECEDENCE

What's an Operator?

To create a formula in 1-2-3 for Windows, you need to use one or more operators. An *operator* is a symbol that instructs 1-2-3 to perform one of the five standard mathematical calculations: addition, subtraction, multiplication, division, and exponentiation.

Operator symbol	Calculation
+	addition
—	subtraction
*	multiplication
/	division
^	exponentiation

1-2-3 calculates operators in a specific order, called *operator precedence*. Exponentiation is always performed first, multiplication and division second, addition and subtraction third. If you're using more than one operator in a formula, you must write your formula using operator precedence so that 1-2-3 knows which operator to calculate first.

Order of Precedence	Operator/s
1	^
2	* /
3	+ -

Operators with lower precedence numbers are performed first in any formula. For example, multiplication is performed before subtraction. If you type in the formula **+A1-B1*5**, 1-2-3 multiplies the contents of cell B1 by 5 (cell B1 is treated as a negative number because of the subtraction operator), and then adds that value to the contents of cell A1, even though you typed the addition and subtraction symbols before the multiplication symbol.

LEARNING THE LINGO

Operator Precedence: The order in which 1-2-3 evaluates mathematical operators in a worksheet formula.

USING OPERATORS AND OPERATOR PRECEDENCE

Sometimes, you need to control the order of precedence for performing calculations. Do this by using parentheses, because operations enclosed in parentheses are always performed first. In the formula **(A2-B2)*5**, 1-2-3 first subtracts the contents of cell B2 from the contents of cell A2, and then multiplies that value by 5.

The results of the formula +A1-B1*5.

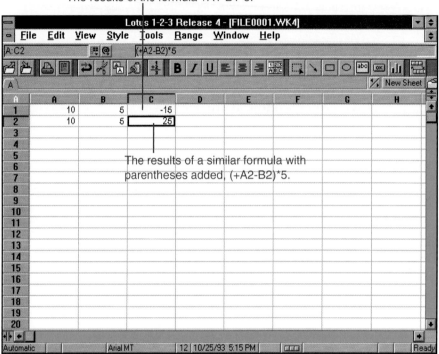

The results of a similar formula with parentheses added, (+A2-B2)*5.

TIP

What if My Formula Contains the Same Precedence Numbers? Operators with the same precedence numbers are performed in a left to right order.

Sample Operators	Result
+8+2*5	18 (The * is performed first, resulting in the value 10; and then the 8 is added.)
(8+2)*5	50 (The parentheses make 1-2-3 calculate + first, resulting in 10; and then the value is multiplied by 5.)

UNDERSTANDING RELATIVE AND ABSOLUTE CELL REFERENCING

What is Relative and Absolute Cell Referencing?

When working with formulas, there are two distinct principles to understand: relative and absolute cell references. A *relative* cell reference is a cell address that is named according to its spatial relationship to the cell containing the formula. For example, if you selected cell A2 and entered the formula +A1, this formula would always refer to "the value in the cell immediately above this cell." If you then copied the formula into another cell, say B2, and then the formula would change as well, becoming +B1. The formula is relative to its location, wherever that might be. By default, all 1-2-3 cell addresses are relative.

On the other hand, there are times when you want the formula to have a fixed reference (refer to a specific cell or cells), no matter where it's moved to. In such a case, you need to designate an absolute cell reference. An *absolute* cell reference is a fixed location. All absolute cell references are denoted by a dollar sign ($) before the column letter and row number in the address ($A$2). For example, if you entered the formula **+$C$1** into cell C2, and then copied the formula to cell D2, the formula would still read **+$C$1**. The formula is fixed to its original location, wherever that might be.

TIP

Careful! Before you move or copy cells that contain formulas, always check the formula to see if absolute cell references are needed.

LEARNING THE LINGO

Relative Cell Reference: A cell address that specifies a location relative to the cell containing the formula.

Absolute Cell Reference: A cell address that specifies a fixed worksheet location.

In this cell, the relative cell reference formula of +A1 is entered.
This formula calculates the contents of the cell above its location.

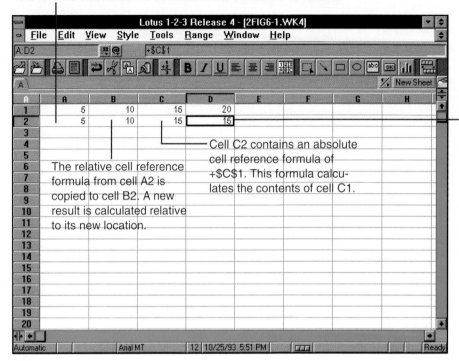

Cell C2 contains an absolute cell reference formula of +$C$1. This formula calculates the contents of cell C1.

The relative cell reference formula from cell A2 is copied to cell B2. A new result is calculated relative to its new location.

The absolute cell reference formula from cell C2 is copied to cell D2. Notice that the result is still that of cell C2. The formula calculates the fixed location, the contents of cell C1.

TIP

An Absolute Shortcut To quickly add dollar signs to make the formula you're typing absolute, press **F4** after you've typed the cell address. 1-2-3 automatically puts the dollar signs into the cell address for you.

USING BUILT-IN FUNCTIONS

What is a Built-In Function?

1-2-3 for Windows has a variety of mathematical functions, called @functions (at functions), that can save you a lot of time. @functions can be used in your worksheet formulas to perform commonly used calculations, or help you with complex calculations. In a nutshell, @functions are pre-set formulas. Instead of going to the trouble of typing in a formula for the data in your worksheet, you can quickly select an @function instead.

An @function can be placed in a cell by itself, or used as part of a formula. Each @function consists of an @ sign and the name of the function, sometimes followed by a parentheses. For example, **@SUM(A1..A5)** is a formula that sums up the values in the range A1..A5. The parentheses enclose a list of mathematical arguments, such as values or cell addresses, that are used in the formula's calculations. You can type in an @function or use the @function selector to enter @functions automatically.

@function selector button ——————— Drop-down list displays the @function menu.

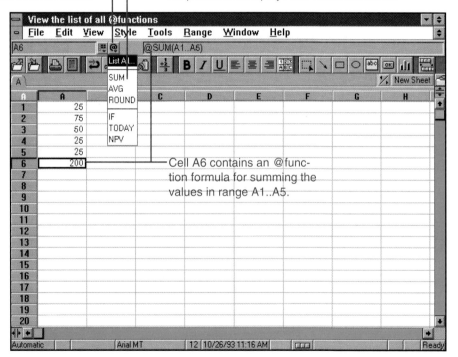

Cell A6 contains an @function formula for summing the values in range A1..A5.

LEARNING THE LINGO

@Function: A formula that is built into 1-2-3.

Argument: Information that tells an @function how or what to calculate.

Creating and Saving Worksheets

USING BUILT-IN FUNCTIONS

The @Function Categories

There are ten @function categories and over 300 @functions to choose from. Obviously, there isn't enough room in this book to show them all, so you should refer to the 1-2-3 for Windows documentation or the Help system for additional information.

@Function Category	Purpose
Calendar	Calculates dates and time values.
Database	Statistical calculations and queries on values in database tables.
Engineering	Performs engineering and advanced mathematical operations.
Financial	Performs financial calculations such as loan payments, investment returns, annuities, and more.
Information	Displays information about cells, ranges, the operating system, and other parts of 1-2-3.
Logical	Calculates the results of logical formulas, such as whether certain conditions in the worksheet are true or false.
Lookup	Searches and finds contents of a cell.
Mathematical	Performs mathematical calculations.
Statistical	Calculates basic statistical operations.
Text	Performs formula operations on labels.

Using the @Function Selector.

1 Select the cell where you want to enter an @function.

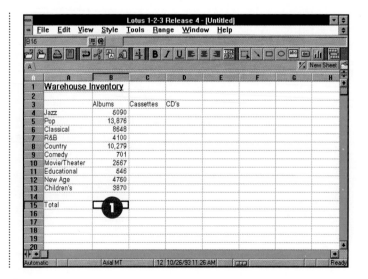

2 Click the @**function selector** button on the Edit line.

3 From the @function menu, select **List All**.

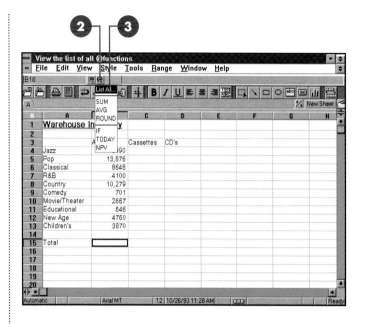

4 When the @Function List dialog box appears, select an @function category from the **Category** drop-down list.

5 Select a function from the @**Functions** list box. Use the scroll arrows to scroll through the list.

6 Click on **OK**, or press **Enter**.

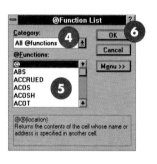

7 The selected function is entered in the cell with placeholders for the required arguments. Type in the argument, such as values, cell addresses, and so on.

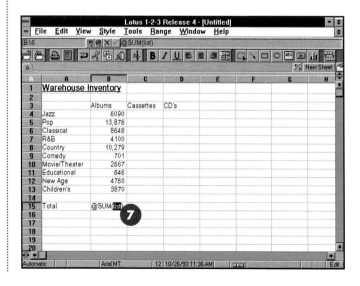

USING BUILT-IN FUNCTIONS

8 Click on the **Confirm** box, or press **Enter**.

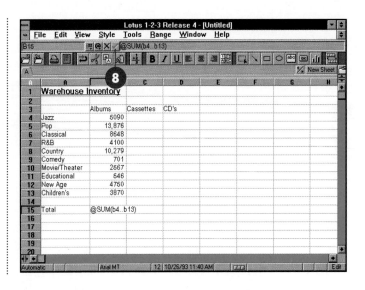

Sample @Function	Result
@SUM(B2..B10)	The sum of all values in the range B2..B10.
@AVG(RAINFALL)	The average of all values in the range named RAINFALL.
@DATE(93,10,26)	The value 34268, which is the date value for October 26, 1993.
@PMT(5000,0.10/12,36)	The monthly payment on $5,000.00 loan, 36-months at 10% annual interest.
@MIN(A:E1..A:E12)	The minimum value in the range A:E1..A:E12.
@MAX(<<REPORT>>SALES)	The maximum value in the named range SALES in the worksheet file REPORT.WK4.

SAVING A WORKSHEET

Why Save Worksheets?

When you're ready to quit the program and you want to keep all your work intact, it's time to save your worksheet. Unless you save your worksheet, everything is "forgotten" by the computer when you turn it off. When you save a worksheet, you can store it on your computer's hard disk or on a floppy disk. When you save your worksheet, or file, you must give it a name.

In 1-2-3 for Windows, the *file name* can be up to eight characters long. File names can be descriptive, such as BUDGET1 or EXPENSES. 1-2-3 automatically adds the file extension .WK4 to all file names (BUDGET1.WK4 or EXPENSES.WK4).

You use the Save **As** command from the **F**ile menu to save your worksheet for the first time. If you're saving an existing worksheet, you can use the **S**ave command from the **F**ile menu.

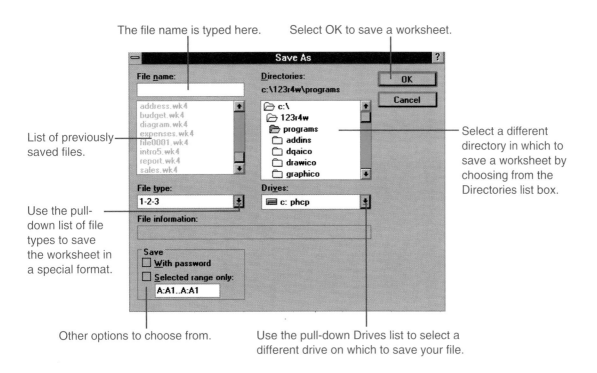

The file name is typed here.   Select OK to save a worksheet.

List of previously saved files.

Use the pull-down list of file types to save the worksheet in a special format.

Select a different directory in which to save a worksheet by choosing from the Directories list box.

Other options to choose from.

Use the pull-down Drives list to select a different drive on which to save your file.

LEARNING THE LINGO

File: Whenever you save a worksheet, the information is saved in a file. Files are given unique names that distinguish them from other files.

File extension: An extra name added to a file name that helps determine what kind of file it is, such as .WK4 (BUDGET.WK4).

SAVING A WORKSHEET

Saving and Naming a Worksheet

1 Click on the File menu, or press **Alt+F**.

2 Click on Save **As**, or press **A**.

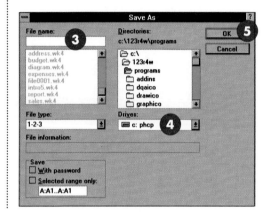

3 Enter a file name for the worksheet.

4 Change the directory, drive, or file type if necessary.

5 Click on **OK**, or press **Enter**.

TIP

Saving Tip It's a good idea to save the worksheet even as you are working on it—and frequently.

If the power goes out and you haven't saved your worksheet, you will lose all your work. Avoid this frustrating experience!

Saving Under Different Directories

1-2-3 for Windows saves your worksheet files automatically in the c:\123R4W directory. If you want to save your worksheet in another directory, select a directory from the Directories list box in the Save As dialog box.

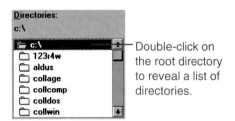

Double-click on the root directory to reveal a list of directories.

What's the Difference Between the Save and the Save As Commands?

The Save As command lets you save your worksheet under a new name. The Save command saves the worksheet under its existing name.

Sometimes, you may want to make slight changes to a worksheet and give the changed worksheet a new name but keep the original intact. The Save As command allows you to do just that. For example, perhaps you have compiled a budget for Department C, and you've named the file DEPTC.WK4. You want to use that same worksheet for compiling a budget for Department D. With the Save As command, you can change the values and save the slightly altered file under a new name, while still retaining the original DEPTC.WK4 file.

On the other hand, if you're simply updating an existing worksheet, the Save command saves the updated worksheet under the original file name by replacing all the data you've changed.

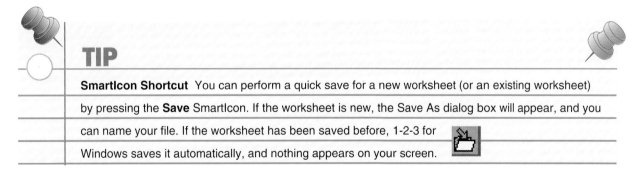

TIP

SmartIcon Shortcut You can perform a quick save for a new worksheet (or an existing worksheet) by pressing the **Save** SmartIcon. If the worksheet is new, the Save As dialog box will appear, and you can name your file. If the worksheet has been saved before, 1-2-3 for Windows saves it automatically, and nothing appears on your screen.

Creating and Saving Worksheets

PART 3

Editing and Printing

This section will teach you how to edit your worksheets, tricks for moving and copying data, the ins and outs of opening and closing worksheets, and finally, how to preview and print your work.

- Editing Data

- Moving and Copying Data

- Opening a Worksheet

- Closing a Worksheet

- Using Print Preview

- Printing a Worksheet

- Page Setup Options

EDITING DATA

What Is Editing?

1-2-3 for Windows gives you the ability to *edit*, or change, your work—what a timesaver! With 1-2-3, you can fix errors and make changes easily. You can delete, replace, or adjust existing worksheet data.

Here are some keys you'll use most often when editing the contents of a worksheet cell:

 Moves the insertion point left one character.

 Moves the insertion point right one character.

HOME Moves the insertion point to the beginning of the data.

END Moves the insertion point to the end of the data.

DELETE Deletes one character to the right of the insertion point.

BACKSPACE Deletes one character to the left of the insertion point.

You can also use the mouse to click anywhere in your data and then use the keyboard keys to make your edits.

TIP

Editing Tricks If you make a mistake while editing a cell, click on the **Cancel** box to restore the original contents.

If you hold down the **Delete** or **Backspace** keys, you can quickly delete more than one character at a time. But be careful; the cursor goes really fast, and you might erase more characters than you intended!

Editing Data in a Cell

1 Double-click on the cell, or press **F2**. The insertion point (cursor), a blinking vertical line, appears at the end of the cell's data.

2 Change your entry using the editing keys on the keyboard. When finished, click on the **Confirm** box, or press **Enter**.

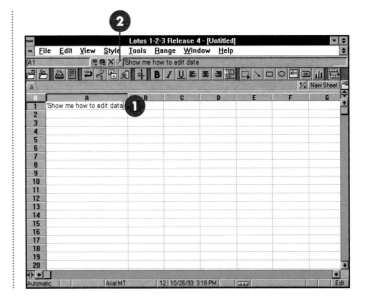

Editing Data in the Contents Box

1 Move the pointer to the cell you want to edit.

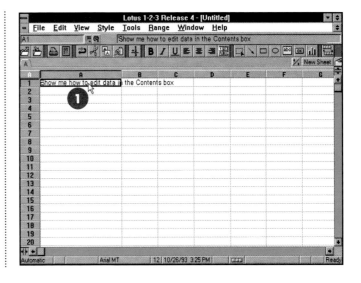

69

EDITING DATA

2 Click on the Contents box. The insertion point, a blinking vertical line, appears where you clicked.

3 Make changes to your entry, use the editing keys on the keyboard to help you. When finished, click on the **Confirm** box, or press **Enter**.

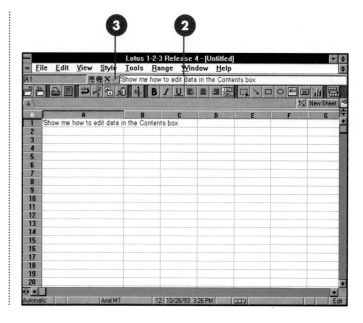

Erasing Data

You can erase the contents or the styles from a cell or range of cells using the **E**dit Cl**e**ar command. First select the cell or range of cells to be erased. Next, select the **E**dit menu, or press **Alt+E**. Then select Cl**e**ar, or press **E**. In the Clear dialog box, choose from the three options available. Click on **OK**, or press **Enter** when finished. You can perform a fast delete by selecting the cell and pressing the **Delete** key. This erases the cell contents only, not the existence of the cell itself.

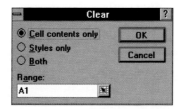

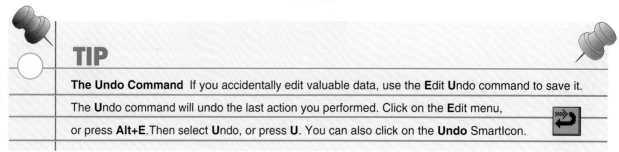

TIP

The Undo Command If you accidentally edit valuable data, use the **E**dit **U**ndo command to save it.

The **U**ndo command will undo the last action you performed. Click on the **E**dit menu,

or press **Alt+E**.Then select **U**ndo, or press **U**. You can also click on the **Undo** SmartIcon.

MOVING AND COPYING DATA

Why Move or Copy Data?

The ability to move and copy cells, ranges, or entire worksheets is a valuable feature of your 1-2-3 for Windows program because it's a lot easier and faster than typing it all again. You can move a formula from one cell to another, copy text from one worksheet to another, all in the brief time it takes for a few mouse clicks or keystrokes.

When data is moved or copied, it's held in a temporary storage area called the *Clipboard*. When you're ready to place the data in another part of your worksheet, it's moved or copied from the Clipboard to your current cell position. You can use the Clipboard to move and copy data to other worksheets, or to other Windows programs.

Another way to copy data is to highlight the cell or range, and then point the mouse pointer at the edge of the range. The mouse pointer becomes a hand icon. Press and hold the **Ctrl** key, press the mouse button, and drag the mouse to bring the pointer to a new location. When the outline of the cell or range is positioned where you want it, release the mouse button. Any existing data is overwritten by the copied data, so be careful.

Don't forget about absolute and relative cell references. Before copying or moving cells that contain formulas, examine the formulas to see if relative or absolute cell references are needed. (See the task "Understanding Relative and Absolute Cell Addressing" in Part 2 for more information.)

Moving and Copying Data

1 Select the data you want to move or copy by highlighting the cell or range containing the data.

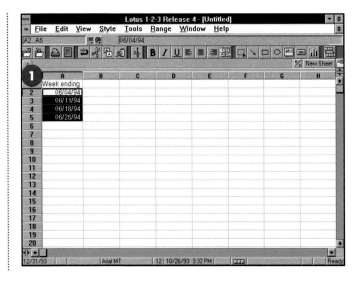

Editing and Printing

MOVING AND COPYING DATA

2 Click on **Edit**, or press **Alt+E**.

3 Click on **Cut**, or press **T** to move data. Or click on **Copy**, or press **C** to copy data.

4 Move the pointer to where you want the cut or copied data to appear.

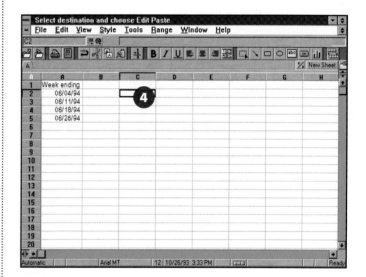

5 Click on **Edit**, or press **Alt+E**.

6 Click on **Paste** or press **P**.

Exercise

Enter the data shown, and then practice copying a range of cells by following these steps:

1 Move the pointer to the beginning of the cell range.

2 Select the entire range. To select with the mouse, press and hold the left mouse button, drag the mouse until the entire range is highlighted, and then release the mouse button. To use the keyboard, press **F4**, and use the arrow keys to highlight the range.

3 Click on **E**dit, or press **Alt+E**.

4 Click on **C**opy, or press **C**.

5 Position the pointer where you want the range copied to.

6 Click on **E**dit, or press **Alt+E**.

7 Click on **P**aste, or press **P**.

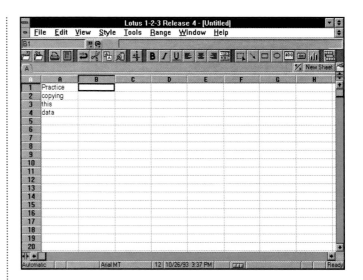

LEARNING THE LINGO

Clipboard: A temporary storage area for data.

Editing and Printing

MOVING AND COPYING DATA

Shortcuts

If you're using the keyboard to enter commands, here are some shortcut keys for cutting, copying, and pasting. Instead of activating the **Edit** menu after selecting cells, press **Ctrl+X** to cut or press **Ctrl+C** to copy; and then press **Ctrl+V** to paste.

If you click on a selected cell or range with the right mouse button, a Quick menu appears displaying the Copy, Cut, and Paste commands. Select the commands you need from the list.

You can perform a quick cut, copy, and paste with the SmartIcon buttons.

 To cut, select the data, and click on the **Cut** icon.

 To copy, select the data, and click on the **Copy** icon.

 To paste, click the cell where the data will be placed, and then click on the **Paste** icon.

OPENING A WORKSHEET

Why Open a Worksheet?

Unless you plan on creating new worksheets every time you work with 1-2-3 for Windows, it's a good idea to learn how to open the worksheets you've saved. The **Open** command, located in the **File** menu, allows you to open files you have previously worked on, as well as files from other directories.

When you select the **Open** command, a dialog box appears with a list of files to open. 1-2-3 displays the **c:\123R4W** directory automatically when you select the **Open** command. You can change directories, locate specific file names, display file types, and change drives. Once you've found the file you're looking for, you can open it and begin working on it again.

Type the name of the worksheet file you want to open in the File name text box.

Select a directory in the Directories list box to open a file in a different directory.

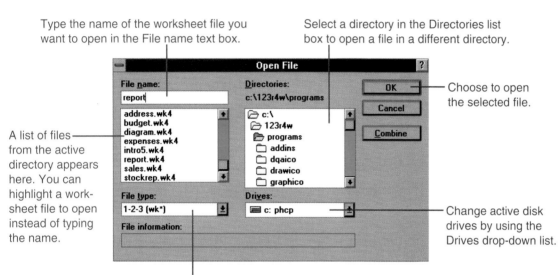

A list of files from the active directory appears here. You can highlight a worksheet file to open instead of typing the name.

Choose to open the selected file.

Change active disk drives by using the Drives drop-down list.

To display specific file types, select from the File type drop-down list.

TIP

Opening Tip When you open another worksheet file without closing the worksheet you were working with, the new file appears in your worksheet window. The old file is there, too—you just can't see it. You can quickly display the Open dialog box by clicking on the **Open**SmartIcon.

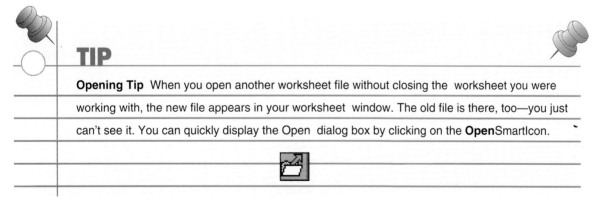

Editing and Printing

OPENING A WORKSHEET

Opening a Worksheet

1 Click on **File**, or press **Alt+F**.

2 Click on **Open**, or press **O**.

3 Select a file name from the list box, or type in the name of the file you want to open.

4 If desired, select from file type, directory, or drive options.

5 Click on **OK**, or press **Enter**.

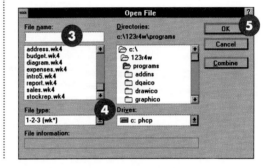

TIP

Opening a New Worksheet File To open a new worksheet in which to work, use the **New** command.

Click on **File**, or press **Alt+F**. Click on **New**, or press **N**. A new worksheet appears in your window.

CLOSING A WORKSHEET

Why Close a Worksheet?

When you are finished working on a worksheet you should close it so you will have more room to work on other worksheets. Closing a worksheet does not close the 1-2-3 for Windows program; it just removes one particular worksheet from your screen.

Closing a Worksheet

1 Click on File, or press **Alt+F**.

2 Click on Close, or press **C**.

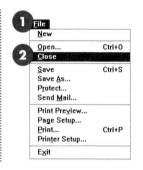

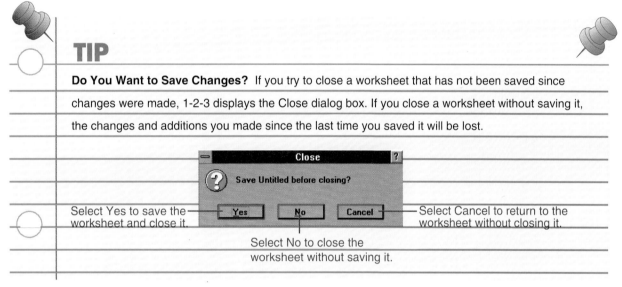

TIP

Do You Want to Save Changes? If you try to close a worksheet that has not been saved since changes were made, 1-2-3 displays the Close dialog box. If you close a worksheet without saving it, the changes and additions you made since the last time you saved it will be lost.

Select Yes to save the worksheet and close it.

Select Cancel to return to the worksheet without closing it.

Select No to close the worksheet without saving it.

USING PRINT PREVIEW

Why Use Print Preview?

Print Preview shows you on-screen what your worksheet data will look when it is printed. You can view one or two entire pages on-screen at the same time, which helps you evaluate the appearance of cells and charts and decide on ways to improve them.

To use Print Preview, select Print Preview from the **File** menu. The Print Preview dialog box appears with options for previewing. Once you have determined which preview options to use, click on **OK**, or press **Enter** to display the Preview screen.

Returns to previous page.

Zooms in to magnify portions of the worksheet.

Moves to next page.

Zooms out to make the page smaller on-screen.

Use to open the Page Setup options.

Prints the worksheet.

Closes the preview window and returns to the worksheet window.

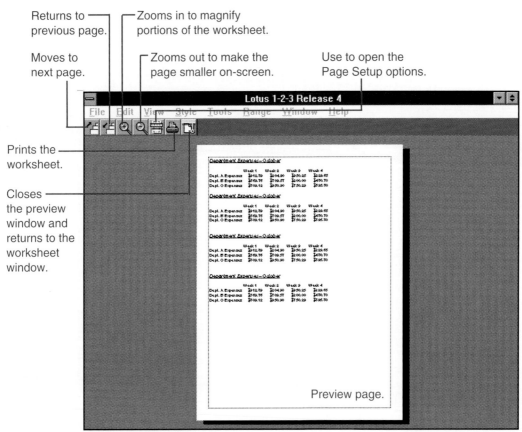

Preview page.

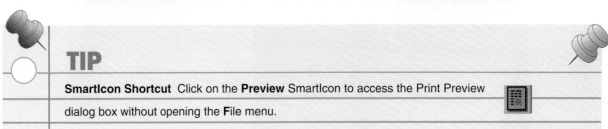

TIP

SmartIcon Shortcut Click on the **Preview** SmartIcon to access the Print Preview dialog box without opening the **File** menu.

Using Print Preview

1 Click on File or press **Alt+F**.

2 Click on Print Preview, or press **V**.

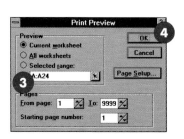

3 Select different options in the Print Preview dialog box, if you want.

4 Click on **OK**, or press **Enter**.

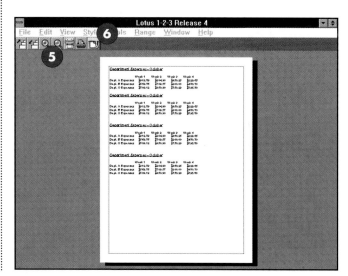

5 Select the **Preview** SmartIcons to view different pages or portions of the worksheet.

6 Click on the **Close** SmartIcon to exit Print Preview, or press **Enter**.

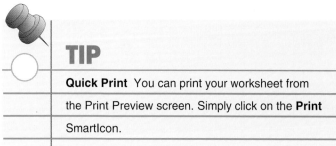

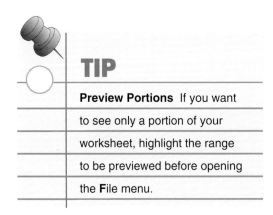

TIP

Preview Portions If you want to see only a portion of your worksheet, highlight the range to be previewed before opening the **F**ile menu.

TIP

Quick Print You can print your worksheet from the Print Preview screen. Simply click on the **Print** SmartIcon.

Editing and Printing

PRINTING A WORKSHEET

When Can a Worksheet Be Printed?

You can print a worksheet at any time, but ordinarily you'll want to print it after you've completed work on it. It's also a good idea to preview your worksheet before you print it, so you can make sure everything looks the way you want it to. Take a look at the "Using Print Preview" task in this section.

When you're finally ready to print, use the **Print** command in the **File** menu. The Print dialog box appears, offering you many printing options. You can control what part of the worksheet to print, what pages to print, and how many copies to print.

For the Print command to work properly, your system must have a printer connected to it. The printer must be turned on, loaded with paper, and set to "on-line." If you encounter difficulties while printing, consult your printer manual.

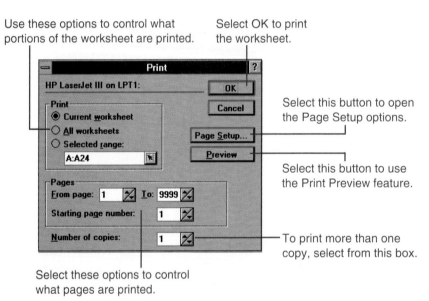

Use these options to control what portions of the worksheet are printed.

Select OK to print the worksheet.

Select this button to open the Page Setup options.

Select this button to use the Print Preview feature.

To print more than one copy, select from this box.

Select these options to control what pages are printed.

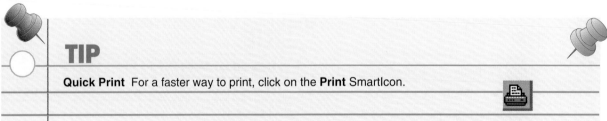

TIP

Quick Print For a faster way to print, click on the **Print** SmartIcon.

80

Printing a Document

1 Click on **File**, or press **Alt+F**.

2 Click on **Print**, or press **P**.

File
- New
- Open...   Ctrl+O
- Close
- Save   Ctrl+S
- Save As...
- Protect...
- Send Mail...
- Print Preview...
- Page Setup...
- Print...   Ctrl+P
- Printer Setup...
- Exit

3 Change printing options (if desired) in the Print dialog box.

4 When you are ready to print, click on **OK**, or press **Enter**.

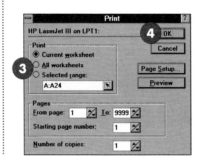

Print
HP LaserJet III on LPT1:

Print
- ● Current worksheet
- ○ All worksheets
- ○ Selected range:
  A:A24

Pages
From page: 1   To: 9999
Starting page number: 1
Number of copies: 1

OK
Cancel
Page Setup...
Preview

TIP

Using Page Setup The Page Setup options, accessed either from the **F**ile menu, the Print Preview window, or the Print dialog box, allow you to change print scaling, margins, orientation, and other print aspects. Turn to the "Page Setup Options" task for more information.

Editing and Printing

PAGE SETUP OPTIONS

What Is Page Setup?

You can use the Page Setup controls to change different aspects of how your page prints. You can control page orientation, margins, scaling, and more. The Page Setup dialog box can be accessed through the File menu, the Print dialog box, and the Print Preview feature.

Select page orientation from these option buttons.

Change margin settings by entering values in inches.

Add a header or footer to your worksheet with these text boxes, or use an Insert SmartIcon.

Insert SmartIcons

Select to save page settings.

Select to retrieve previously saved page settings.

Change the default settings with these buttons.

Select from this drop-down list to change the scaling of your printout.

Any or all of these options can be included in the printout.

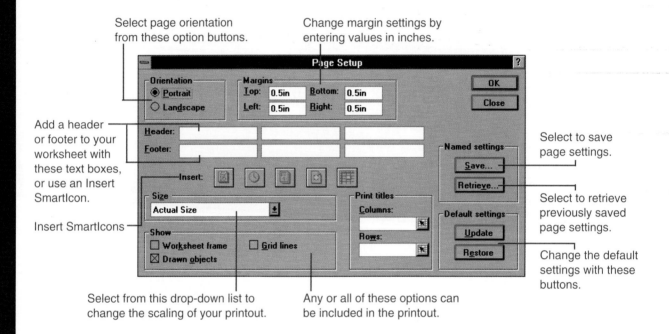

LEARNING THE LINGO

Header: Text or other data that can be repeated at the top of every worksheet page.

Footer: Text or other data that can be repeated at the bottom of every worksheet page.

PART 4

Formatting Your Worksheet

In this section, you will learn how to make your worksheet data look good. You'll discover techniques for adding borders, changing fonts, adjusting row height and column width, and more. Each task teaches a skill that helps you create professional-looking reports that present your data with style.

- Formatting Data

- Working with Fonts

- Changing Alignment

- Changing Column Width and Row Height

- Adding Borders

- Working with Styles

FORMATTING DATA

What Is Formatting?

Formatting refers to the way your worksheet data looks, such as positioning, fonts, sizes, and styles. You can use formatting to emphasize certain parts of your worksheet and to improve its appearance. Formatting can be specified before you begin typing data or it can be applied to existing data. Through careful selection and combination of the various formatting options, you can improve the readability and presentation of your worksheets.

Formatting numbers includes how the numbers are displayed. For example, perhaps you want several decimal points, a dollar sign, and separators for thousands. The Number Format options let you control how numeric values are displayed in your worksheet.

Hidden format: The cell appears blank, and the data appears in the Contents box.

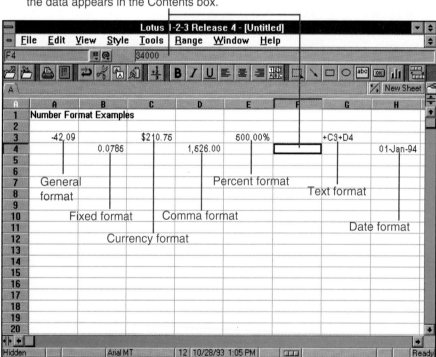

Format	Description
General format	Displays numbers with as many decimal places as needed. Negative numbers are displayed with a minus sign.
Fixed format	Allows you to designate the number of decimal places displayed.
Currency format	Displays numbers with a currency symbol, thousands separators, and designated decimal places.
Comma format	Displays numbers the same as currency format, without the currency symbol.
Percent format	Displays numbers multiplied by 100 with a percent sign. You can designate how many decimal places are shown.
Hidden format	Displays no data in the cell, but when the cell is active, the data appears in the Contents box. Use this format to protect sensitive data.
Text format	Displays the formula instead of the results of the formula.
Date and Time format	Allows you to display date and time numbers in a variety of formats.
Automatic format	The default format 1-2-3 uses until you specify another format. Automatic format displays numbers based on the symbol you use when entering the data. For example, if you type a percent sign, 1-2-3 automatically uses the Percent format.

LEARNING THE LINGO

Font: A set of characters with a specific design.

Formatting Your Worksheet

FORMATTING DATA

Changing Number Formats

1 Select the cell or range to apply or change formatting.

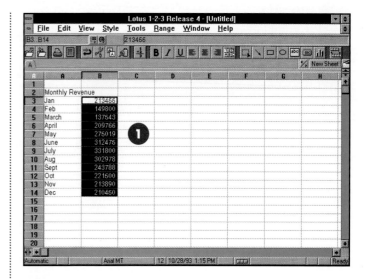

2 Click on **Style**, or press **Alt+S**.

3 Click on **Number Format**, or press **N**.

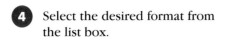

4 Select the desired format from the list box.

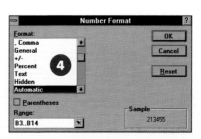

5 If you select Fixed, Scientific, Currency, Comma, or Percent formats, the Decimal Places text box appears. Click on the up or down arrows, or type in a value to enter the number of decimal places you want displayed.

6 Click on **OK**, or press **Enter**.

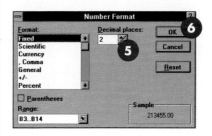

86

Quick Decimal Formatting

Click on the Format or Decimal Place indicators on the status bar to make quick
formatting changes to a selected cell or range.

Decimal Place indicator

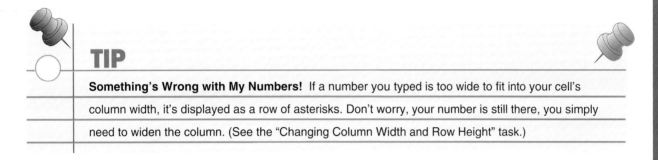

Format indicator

TIP

Something's Wrong with My Numbers! If a number you typed is too wide to fit into your cell's

column width, it's displayed as a row of asterisks. Don't worry, your number is still there, you simply

need to widen the column. (See the "Changing Column Width and Row Height" task.)

Formatting Your Worksheet

WORKING WITH FONTS

What Are Fonts?

Fonts, also called typestyles or typefaces, are an important part of your worksheet formatting. A font is a set of characters with a specific design and point size. You can use different fonts with your worksheet data, both numbers and text, to increase the clarity and visual appeal of your work. Each font is identified by its own name, such as Times Roman, Arial, or Helvetica. Each font is also available in several different sizes, which are measured in points (72 points is equal to one inch). Special attributes, such as bold, italics, or underlining, can also be added to enhance your data even more.

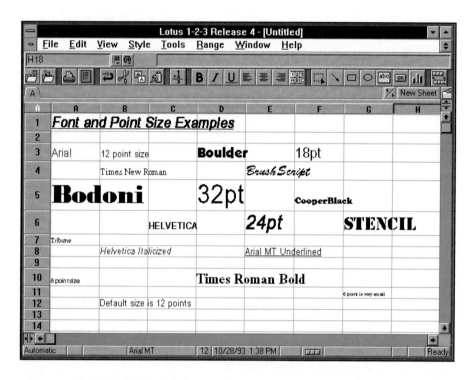

LEARNING THE LINGO

Point Size: The measurement of font size in height. 1 point measures 1/72-inch.

Changing Fonts

1 Select the cell or range in which you want to change or apply the font.

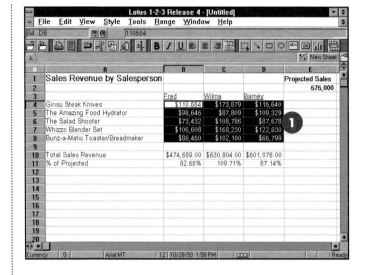

2 Click on Style, or press **Alt+S**.

3 Click on Font & Attributes, or press **F**.

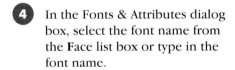

4 In the Fonts & Attributes dialog box, select the font name from the **F**ace list box or type in the font name.

5 Select a font size from the **S**ize list box, or type in a size value.

6 Choose any special attributes from the Attributes options.

7 If desired, choose a font color from the **C**olor drop-down list.

8 Look at the Sample box to see how the selected font and attributes will appear.

9 Click on **OK**, or press **Enter**.

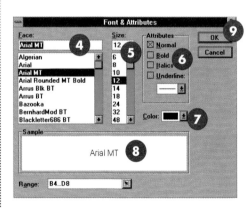

Formatting Your Worksheet

WORKING WITH FONTS

Change the Default Font

You can change the default font that 1-2-3 uses automatically. Select the **St**yle menu, and then choose **W**orksheet Defaults. In the dialog box, select a new font name from the **F**ace list. You can also change the default font size, too. When finished, click on **OK**, or press **Enter**. The new default font will be used for all cells from this point except those you change to something else or unless you are in a new worksheet.

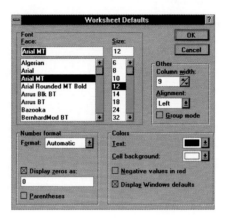

Formatting

Click on the Font or Size indicators on the status bar to quickly change the formatting of a selected cell or range.

Size indicator

Font indicator

Use the attributes SmartIcons to quickly change data to bold, italics, or underline.

Bold   Italics   Underline

CHANGING COLUMN WIDTH AND ROW HEIGHT

Why Change Column Width or Row Height?

By default, 1-2-3's worksheet columns are set up with a fixed width, and rows
have a fixed height. However, some of your worksheet data may not fit into those
fixed measurements. For example, labels that are too wide for a column will overlap the column to the right, or only a portion of the label will be visible. When
numbers do not fit, a row of asterisks is displayed. In such cases, you'll need to
adjust the column width or row height.

Labels that won't fit the default
width overlap other columns.

Adjusted columns to fit data.

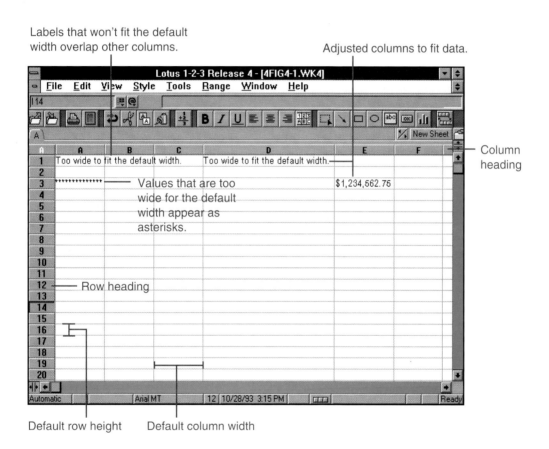

Column heading

Values that are too wide for the default width appear as asterisks.

Row heading

Default row height   Default column width

Formatting Your Worksheet

CHANGING COLUMN WIDTH AND ROW HEIGHT

Changing Column Width

1 Select the cell or range in the column you want to adjust.

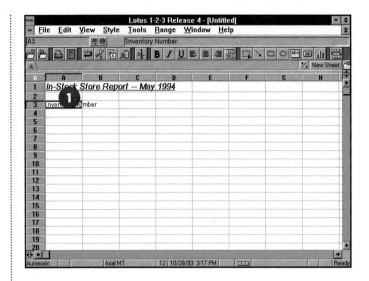

2 Click on **S**tyle, or press **Alt+S**.

3 Click on **C**olumn Width, or press **C**.

4 When the Column Width dialog box appears, specify a new column width in the **S**et width to characters box. Click on the arrows, or type in a value.

5 Select the **F**it Widest Entry option to have 1-2-3 automatically adjust the column width to the longest entry.

6 To reset the column widths to the 1-2-3 default, select the **R**eset to worksheet default option.

7 Click on **OK**, or press **Enter**.

Changing Row Height

1 Select the cell or range in the row you want to adjust.

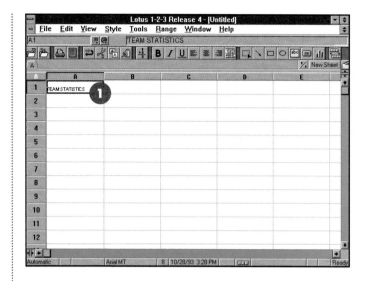

2 Click on **Style**, or press **Alt+S**.

3 Click on **R**ow Height, or press **R**.

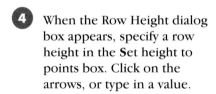

4 When the Row Height dialog box appears, specify a row height in the **S**et height to points box. Click on the arrows, or type in a value.

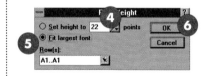

5 Select the **F**it largest font option to have 1-2-3 automatically adjust the row height to the tallest entry.

6 Click on **OK**, or press **Enter**.

Formatting Your Worksheet

CHANGING COLUMN WIDTH AND ROW HEIGHT

Change Your Columns or Rows with a Move of the Mouse!

You can quickly adjust column widths or row heights by dragging your mouse. Move your mouse pointer to the column or row heading you want to adjust. Point at the heading border, and the pointer becomes a double-headed arrow. Press and hold the left mouse button, drag the pointer to the desired width or height, and then release the mouse button.

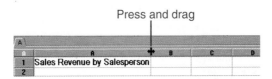

Press and drag

To change several rows and columns at once, highlight the cells or range, and then drag the column or row heading border to a new position.

ADDING BORDERS

What Can I Do with Borders?

Add borders and frames to your worksheet to set off different areas of data, or emphasize values and labels. You can place borders and frames around cells and ranges, around each individual cell, or along certain edges. All the border and frame options are available in the Lines & Color dialog box. You can even add background colors and shading to your data.

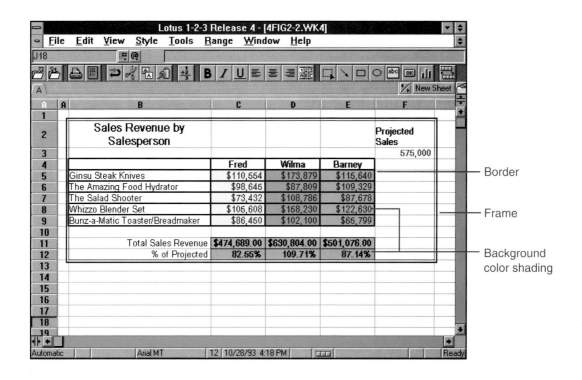

ADDING BORDERS

Adding a Border

1 Select the cell or range to which you want to add a border.

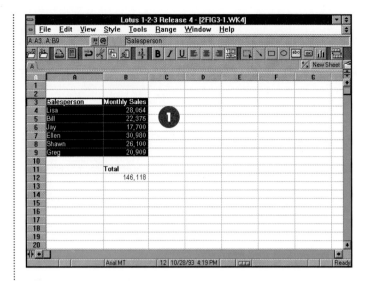

2 Click on **Style**, or press **Alt+S**.

3 Click on **Lines & Color**, or press **L**.

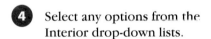

4 Select any options from the Interior drop-down lists.

5 Select any combination of borders from the Border options.

6 Choose border line types and color from the drop-down lists.

7 View your border selections in the Sample box.

8 Click **OK**, or press **Enter**.

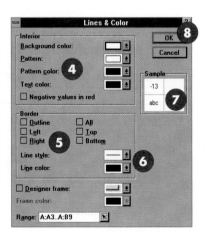

Add Designer Frames

Select the **D**esigner frame option in the Lines & Color dialog box to add frames to your cells or ranges. Use the **D**esigner frame drop-down list to choose a style. Use the Frame color drop-down list to change colors.

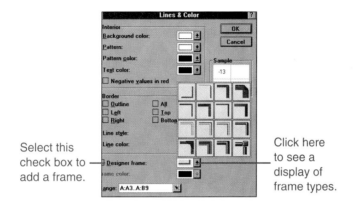

Select this check box to add a frame.

Click here to see a display of frame types.

Paint Your Interior

Use the Interior options in the Lines & Colors dialog box to add background colors, shading, and change the color of text. Of course, you'll need a color printer to output your color selections.

Choose shading options from the Interior selections.

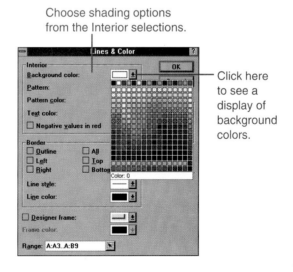

Click here to see a display of background colors.

Formatting Your Worksheet

WORKING WITH STYLES

What Are Styles?

Styles are predefined sets of formatting commands that you can apply to your worksheet. They're very convenient to use, and save you the effort of choosing formatting commands each time. Styles have assigned names and are saved so you can use them again and again. 1-2-3 for Windows comes with ten predefined styles, and you can also make your own. Styles can include number formats, colors, fonts and attributes, alignment, and borders.

Creating a Style

1 Select the cell or range that contains the formatting you want to save for future use.

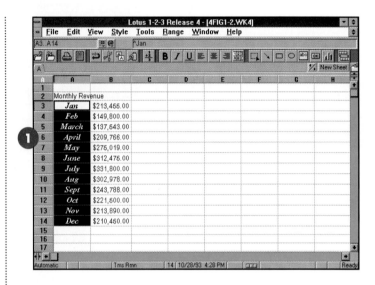

2 Click on **Style**, or press **Alt+S**.

3 Click on Named **Style**, or press **S**.

4 In the Named Style dialog box, type a name in the Style **name** text box. The name can be as long as 15 characters.

5 Click on **D**efine, or press **Alt+D**.

6 Click **OK**, or press **Enter**.

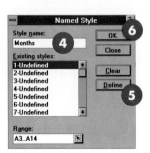

98

Applying a Style

1 Select the cell or range to which to add a style.

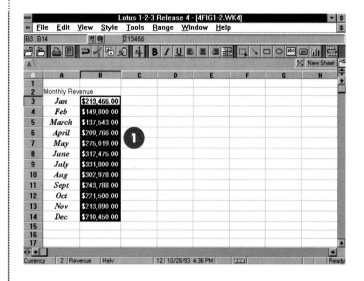

2 Click on Style, or press **Alt+S**.

3 Click on Named Style, or press **S**.

4 In the Named Style dialog box, select the desired style name from the **Existing Styles** list.

5 Click **OK**, or press **Enter**.

TIP

Faster Styles Use the **Style** button on the status bar to quickly assign a style to a selected cell or range. Click on the button, and then click on the style name from the list.

Style button.

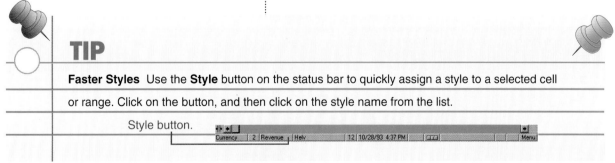

Formatting Your Worksheet

PART 5

Beyond the Basics

This last part of the book introduces some additional 1-2-3 features that can help you work with your data. You will learn to make charts based on your worksheet input, move the charts around, and add enhancements. You will also learn about graphics, and using your worksheet as a database to organize your data.

- Creating a Chart
- Moving and Resizing a Chart
- Adding Chart Enhancements
- Changing a Chart's Axis
- Using Graphics
- Creating a Database
- Sorting a Database
- Searching a Database

CREATING A CHART

Why Make Charts?

Charts are extremely useful for visually summing up your worksheet data. 1-2-3 for Windows offers a variety of chart types to choose from. All 1-2-3 charts are based on *data series*. A data series is a group of worksheet labels or values that are displayed together in the same column or row. Charts are built with data series on an X-axis (horizontal) and a Y-axis (vertical). The X-axis usually contains labels that identify the data by category, such as Months, Regions, States, and so on. The Y-axis always contains values, and there can be up to 23 Y data series on a chart.

Once a chart has been created, it's displayed in the worksheet at a location you designate. You can even display a chart on top of other worksheet data—the data is still there, but it is hidden. Any time you want to make adjustments to your chart, you must select it, as you do with other 1-2-3 elements. Move the mouse pointer over the chart border, and click. When selected, the chart displays small black boxes on its border. After you've made a few charts, you'll be amazed at how easy it is to add visual impact to your worksheet.

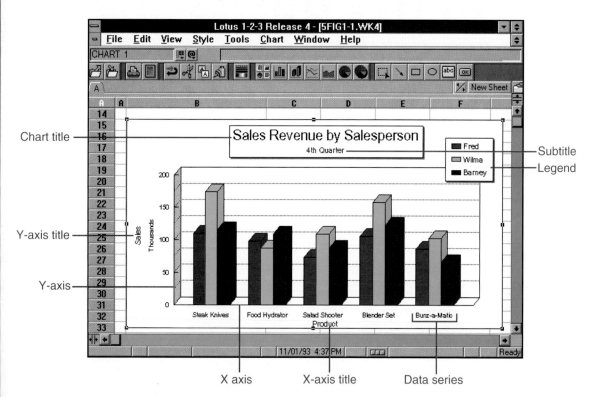

Chart Type	Description
Line	Plots data values as points or symbols, and connects them with a line. Useful for illustrating changes that occur over time.
Area	A line chart that plots data series stacked on each other, with shading filling in the areas in between the lines. Area charts are good for illustrating trends over time.
Bar	Displays values as vertical rectangular bars that rise up from the X-axis. The height of each bar is proportional to the corresponding value on the Y-axis. Useful for comparing totals for several categories.
Pie	Uses only a single Y data series. Plotted in a circle, with the circle representing a total value, and wedges representing portions of the total value. Useful for showing contributions to a whole.
XY	Also called a scatter chart, this type plots values on the X-axis. Useful for showing relational or correlating sets of values.
HLCO	High-low-close-open. A specialized chart that is used to display stock market data.
Mixed	A combination of line, area, and bar chart types in one chart.
Radar	A line chart that stems from a central point. Radar charts are good for showing symmetry of data.
3D Line	A line chart plotted in a three-dimensional perspective.
3D Area	An area chart displayed in a three-dimensional perspective.
3D Bar	A bar chart plotted in a three-dimensional perspective.
3D Pie	A pie chart displayed in a three-dimensional perspective.

Beyond the Basics

CREATING A CHART

Creating a Chart

 1 Select the worksheet data to be charted. Include a data series for labels to be plotted on the X-axis, and a data series for values to be plotted on the Y-axis.

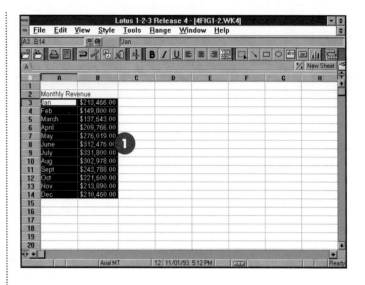

 2 Click on Tools, or press **Alt+T**.

 3 Click on Chart, or press **C**.

TIP

Custom-Made Charts   To custom size your chart (if you don't want to settle for the default size), drag the mouse instead of clicking in step 4. Move your mouse pointer to where you want the upper left corner of the chart, and press and hold the left mouse button while dragging diagonally to the bottom right corner of where you want the chart. Release the mouse button, and continue with the rest of the steps for creating a chart.

4 The mouse pointer changes to a small chart symbol. Click on the location on the worksheet where you want the upper left corner of the chart to go. A default size bar chart is created by 1-2-3.

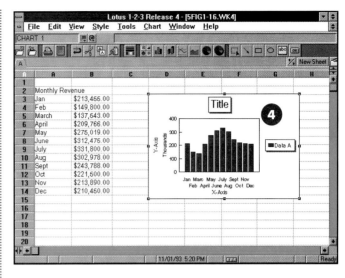

5 To change chart types, make sure the chart is selected by clicking on it, and then click on Chart, or press **Alt+C**. (The **R**ange menu on the main menu bar changed its name to Chart when you inserted and selected a chart. It changes back to the **R**ange menu name when the chart is no longer selected.)

6 Click on **T**ype, or press **T**.

7 In the Type dialog box, choose the desired chart type.

8 Select a chart orientation.

9 Click on one of the style samples displayed.

10 Click on **OK**, or press **Enter**.

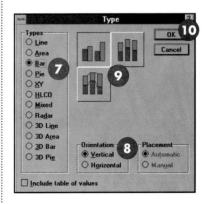

LEARNING THE LINGO

Legend: A key that identifies a chart's data.

Axis: A horizontal or vertical line that build a chart's measurable and comparative data.

Plot: The way data is displayed inside a chart's axes.

Beyond the Basics

CREATING A CHART

Charting Rules

Because of the nature of charts and their levels of complexity, 1-2-3 follows certain rules in interpreting the data. These rules allow 1-2-3 to guess as accurately as possible how you want your chart to look. The rules are based on the relative number of rows and columns in the selected range of chart data.

Rule #1: *If the range contains more rows than columns, 1-2-3 groups the data into a data series by columns.* The first column is the X series, all other columns of data are the Y series. For example, if you selected the range A2..C10, the data in column A would become the X series on the X-axis of your chart. Columns B, and C would become the Y series of data on the Y-axis of your chart. Any labels at the top of the Y range columns are used for the legend labels. Blank rows and columns are ignored.

Rule #2: *If the range contains more columns than rows (or an equal number), 1-2-3 groups the data into a data series by rows.* The first row is treated as the X series, and the other rows are the Y series. For example, if you selected the range A2..G5, the data in row 2 would become the X series on the X-axis of your chart. Rows 3, 4, and 5 would become the Y series of data on the Y-axis of your chart. Any labels to the left of the Y range rows are used for the legend labels. Blank rows and columns are ignored.

Rule #3: *If the selected range contains labels to the left of the data or above the data, 1-2-3 uses them to create the title, subtitle, and legend labels.*

Saving and Printing Charts

Charts are automatically saved when you save your worksheet file. No special action is required. Printing is just as effortless: click on the Print icon, or select File Print. In the Print dialog box, make sure that the Selected chart option button is on. Then click on OK, or press Enter to print.

Make sure this option is turned on:

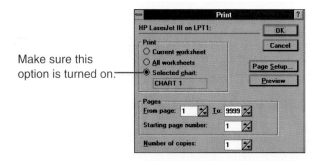

TIP

Getting Rid of Charts To quickly delete a chart you've created, select it, and press the **Delete** key.

MOVING AND RESIZING A CHART

Why Move or Resize Charts?

As you edit your worksheet, you may need to reposition a chart so it appears in another area of your worksheet, or perhaps you would like to make the chart bigger to give it greater emphasis. With 1-2-3 for Windows, you can easily move and resize your charts to other positions on your worksheet.

Moving a Chart

1 Select the chart to be moved.

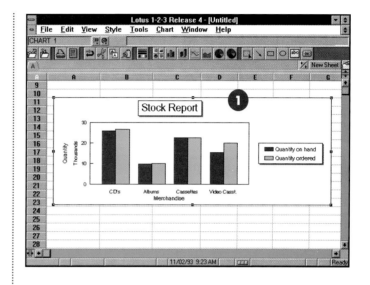

2 Click on **Edit**, or press **Alt+E**.

3 Click on **Cut**, or press **T**.

4 Move the pointer to the work-sheet location where you want to place the upper left corner of the chart.

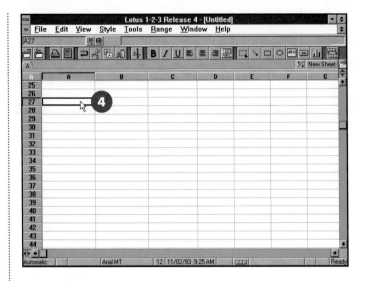

5 Click on **Edit**, or press **Alt+E**.

6 Click on **Paste**, or press **P**.

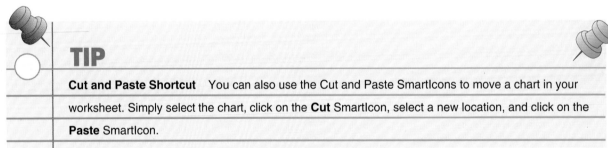

TIP

Cut and Paste Shortcut   You can also use the Cut and Paste SmartIcons to move a chart in your worksheet. Simply select the chart, click on the **Cut** SmartIcon, select a new location, and click on the **Paste** SmartIcon.

Resizing a Chart

1 Select the chart to be resized.

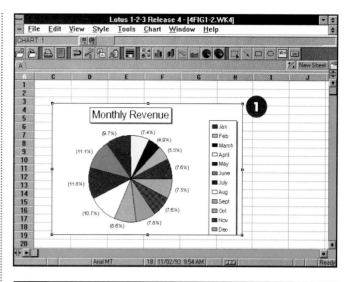

2 Point the mouse pointer at one of the small black rectangles on the chart's border until the mouse pointer changes to a double-headed arrow.

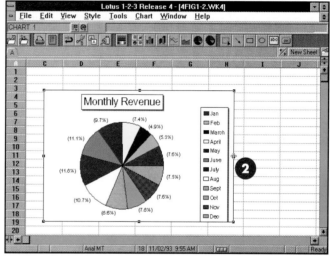

3 Press the left mouse button, and drag the chart outline to the desired shape and size, releasing the button when finished.

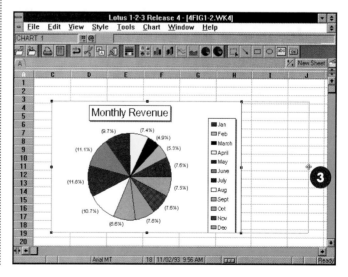

Beyond the Basics

ADDING CHART ENHANCEMENTS

What Are Chart Enhancements?

Chart enhancements include additional modifications you can make to a chart to improve its appearance, readability, and impact. You can add titles and footnotes, a legend to explain how to read the chart data, and, of course, any formatting, such as fonts, font attributes, sizes, and positioning.

Titles

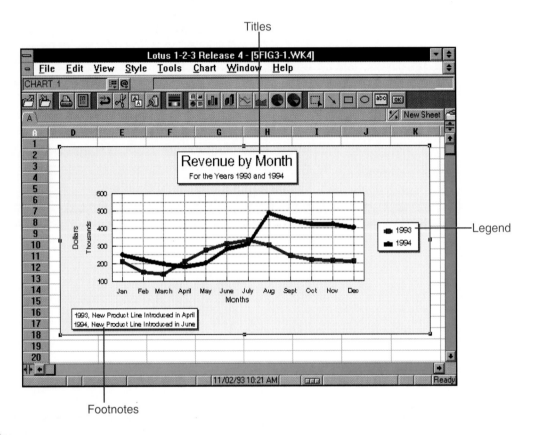

Footnotes

Legend

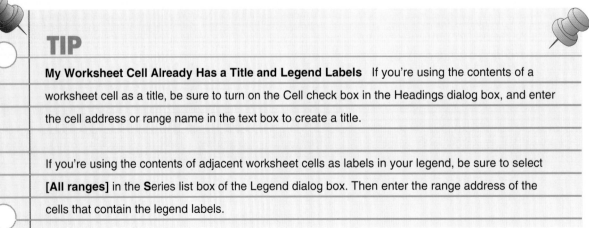

TIP

My Worksheet Cell Already Has a Title and Legend Labels If you're using the contents of a worksheet cell as a title, be sure to turn on the Cell check box in the Headings dialog box, and enter the cell address or range name in the text box to create a title.

If you're using the contents of adjacent worksheet cells as labels in your legend, be sure to select **[All ranges]** in the **S**eries list box of the Legend dialog box. Then enter the range address of the cells that contain the legend labels.

Adding Titles and Footnotes

1 Select the chart to which you want to add titles or footnotes.

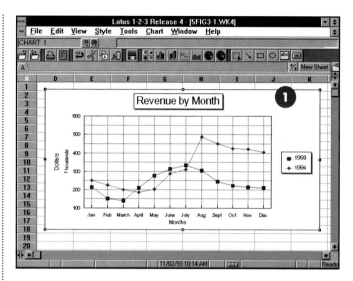

2 Click on **Chart**, or press **Alt+C**.

3 Click on **Headings**, or press **H**.

4 In the Title section of the Headings dialog box, enter the chart's main title in Line **1** and the subtitle in Line **2**.

5 Choose a title placement from the Placement options.

6 To enter a footnote, enter the footnote in Line **1** of the Note section.

7 Click on **OK**, or press **Enter**.

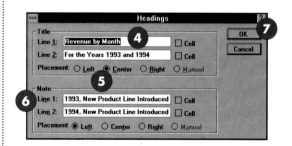

Beyond the Basics

ADDING CHART ENHANCEMENTS

Adding a Legend

1 Select the chart.

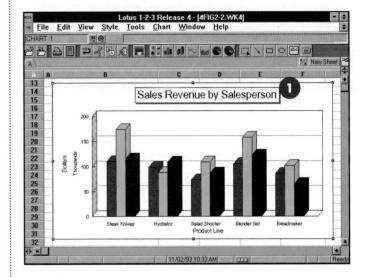

2 Click on **Chart**, or press **Alt+C**.

3 Click on **Legend**, or press **L**.

4 In the Legend dialog box, select a data series to identify with a legend.

5 Enter the legend label for the selected data series in the **Legend entry** text box. Repeat steps 4 and 5 for any additional data series.

6 Select a placement option under the Place legend section.

7 Click on **OK**, or press **Enter**.

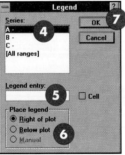

CHANGING A CHART'S AXIS

Why Change the Axis of a Chart?

Changing your chart's axis can also enhance the presentation of your worksheet data. You can add titles to each axis, including a unit title that describes the numerical measurements on a chart axis. You can also change the axis scale, which adjusts the increments at which values are displayed on the axis. The axis scale is only adjustable to the Y-axis on most charts.

LEARNING THE LINGO

Axis scale: The maximum and minimum values displayed on a chart's axis.

Adding Axis Titles

1 Select the chart to modify.

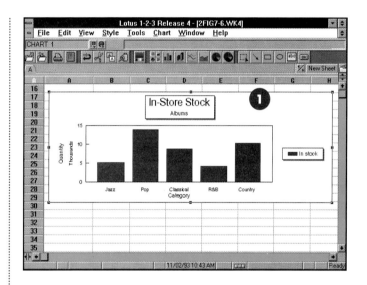

2 Click on **Chart**, or press **Alt+C**.

3 Click on **Axis**, or press **A**.

Beyond the Basics

CHANGING A CHART'S AXIS

4 Select the axis to add a title to.

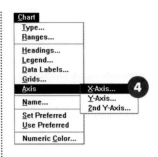

5 When the axis dialog box appears, enter the desired title in the Axis title text box.

6 Click on **OK**, or press **Enter**.

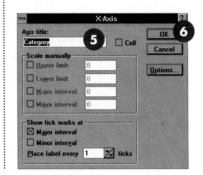

Changing Unit Titles

To modify the unit titles, or increments on a chart's axis, select the **Options** button in the X-Axis or Y-Axis dialog box in step 5. The Options dialog box appears. Under Axis units, select Automatic to have 1-2-3 determine the exponent to use, or select Manual to enter your own exponent. Under Units title, select Automatic to have 1-2-3 create a unit title based on the exponent used, or select Manual to enter your own unit title and type it in the text box. (You can also click on the Cell check box and enter a cell address of the title you want to use.)

TIP

Using a Worksheet Cell Label?

If you're using a worksheet cell label as a title, turn on the Cell check box in the Axis dialog box, and enter the cell's address or range name in the Axis title text box.

TIP

Three Types of Axis Scales   You can control the range of values on your chart's axis with the type of axis scale you use. A *standard scale* arranges numbers in a linear fashion. A *logarithmic scale* arranges numbers logarithmically. A *100% scale* displays values from 0% to 100% that represent percentages instead of absolute values.

Changing an Axis Scale

1 Select the chart.

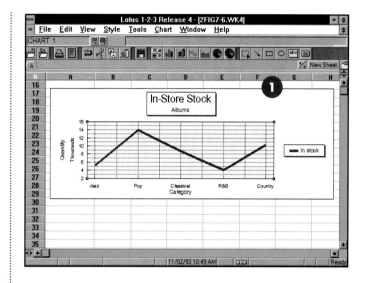

2 Click on **Chart**, or press **Alt+C**.

3 Click on **Axis**, or press **A**.

4 Select the axis to be modified.

5 In the axis dialog box, click on the **Options** button or press **Alt+O**.

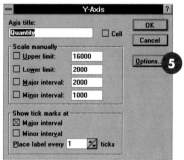

Beyond the Basics

115

CHANGING A CHART'S AXIS

6 Choose the type of scale to use from the Type of scale drop-down list.

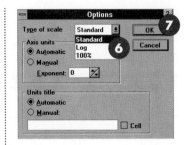

7 Click on **OK**, or press **Enter**.

8 In the axis dialog box, turn on the Upper limit and Lower limit check boxes, and enter the desired axis limits in the text boxes.

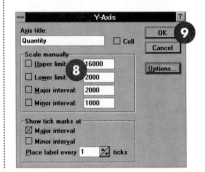

9 Click on **OK**, or press **Enter**.

Help—The Scale is All Wrong!

You can easily return an axis to automatic scaling. Select the chart, and then select the Chart menu. Next, select **Axis** and the specific axis to be changed. When the axis dialog box is displayed, turn off the Upper limit and Lower limit check boxes. Click on **OK**, or press **Enter** when finished.

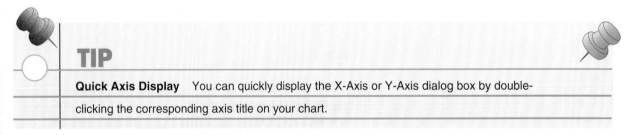

TIP

Quick Axis Display   You can quickly display the X-Axis or Y-Axis dialog box by double-clicking the corresponding axis title on your chart.

What Are Graphics?

Graphics are objects that you draw in your 1-2-3 worksheet. Graphics include lines, arrows, shapes, and text blocks. Lines and arrows can be used to draw attention to important points in your worksheet. Shapes can be used to add circles and squares around your worksheet data. Text blocks are rectangular sections of text that can be placed anywhere on a worksheet. Use them to make notes and captions.

LEARNING THE LINGO

Graphics: Objects that can be drawn in the 1-2-3 worksheet. Graphics include lines, shapes, arrows, and text blocks.

USING GRAPHICS

Drawing Lines, Arcs, and Arrows

1 Select **Tools**, or press **Alt+T**.

2 Select **Draw**, or press **D**.

3 Select **Line**, **Arc**, or **Arrow**.

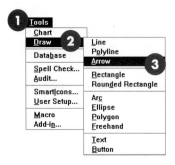

4 Move the mouse pointer to the position in your worksheet where you want to begin the graphic.

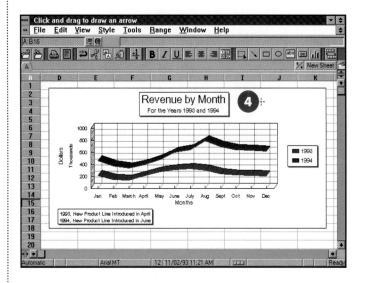

5 Press and hold the left mouse button, and drag the mouse pointer to the end position of the area you want the graphic to fill. Release the mouse button when finished.

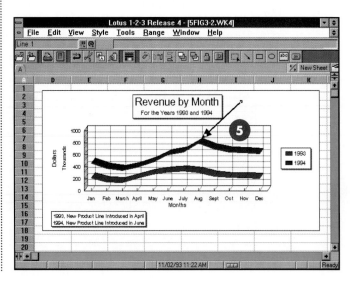

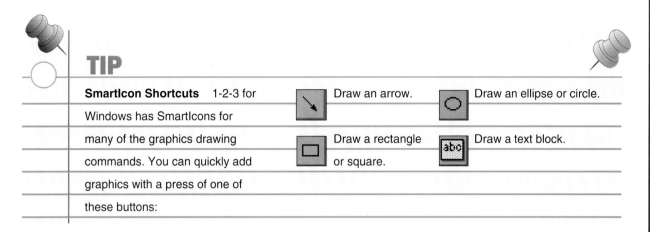

TIP

SmartIcon Shortcuts 1-2-3 for Windows has SmartIcons for many of the graphics drawing commands. You can quickly add graphics with a press of one of these buttons:

Draw an arrow.

Draw an ellipse or circle.

Draw a rectangle or square.

Draw a text block.

Drawing Shapes

1 Select Tools, or press **Alt+T**.

2 Select Draw, or press **D**.

3 Select a shape from the list: **R**ectangle, Roun**d**ed Rectangle, or **E**llipse.

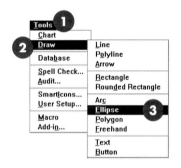

4 Move the mouse pointer to the location on your worksheet where you want the shape to start.

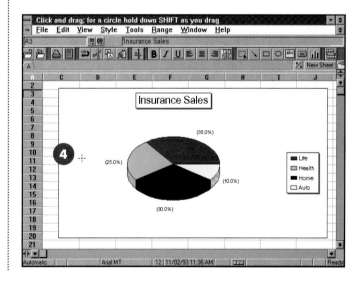

Beyond the Basics

USING GRAPHICS

5 Press the left mouse button, and drag the pointer to the desired size and shape. Release the mouse button when finished.

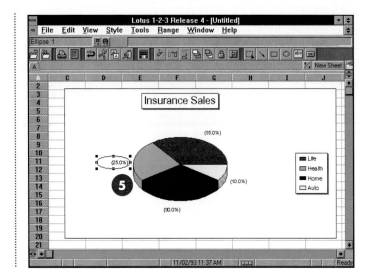

TIP

Ship Shape Tips   To draw a circle instead of an ellipse, or a square instead of a rectangle, press and hold the **Shift** key while dragging the mouse in step 5.

Adding a Text Block

1 Select **Tools**, or press **Alt+T**.

2 Select **Draw**, or press **D**.

3 Select **Text**, or press **T**.

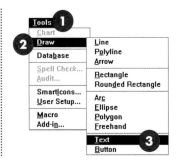

4 Move the mouse pointer to the location on your worksheet where you want the text box to begin.

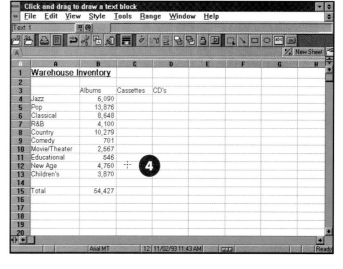

5 Press the left mouse button, drag the block outline to the desired size, and then release the mouse button.

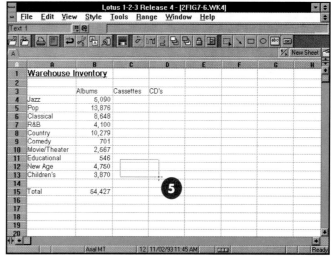

6 Type in the text you want to appear in the text box. When finished, click anywhere outside the box.

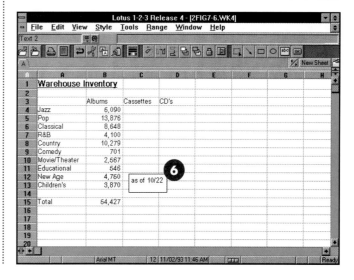

Beyond the Basics

USING GRAPHICS

Changing Graphic Objects

To make changes to any graphic object, you must first select it. Click on the object, and small squares, called *handles*, appear on the object's borders. To delete a graphic object, select the object, and press the **Delete** key. To move a graphic, point anywhere on the object *except the handles*, and drag it to a new location. To resize a graphic object, point and drag one of its handles. You can also use the move and resize features explained in the task "Moving and Resizing a Chart".

You can change the thickness, color, and pattern of a graphic's line. Move the mouse pointer to the object, and right-click to display the Quick menu. Select Lines & Color from the menu list. When the Lines & Color dialog box appears, make the desired selections. Click on **OK**, or press **Enter** when finished.

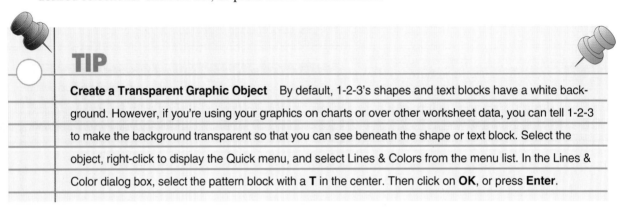

TIP

Create a Transparent Graphic Object   By default, 1-2-3's shapes and text blocks have a white background. However, if you're using your graphics on charts or over other worksheet data, you can tell 1-2-3 to make the background transparent so that you can see beneath the shape or text block. Select the object, right-click to display the Quick menu, and select Lines & Colors from the menu list. In the Lines & Color dialog box, select the pattern block with a **T** in the center. Then click on **OK**, or press **Enter**.

CREATING A DATABASE

What's a Database?

A *database* is a collection of organized information with a uniform structure, such as a mailing list, or an inventory of merchandise. For example, an address database may include categories for name, address, city, state, and zip code. Each entry in a database has the same structure, arranged into fields and records.

A database *record* is one complete database entry. A *field* is one part of a database record, a name category for example. All entries in a given field should be of the same type, either labels or values, not a mix of both. Naturally, the row and column grid setup in 1-2-3 for Windows is perfectly suited for compiling database information. Each field has its own column, and each record has its own row.

Before you create a database, it's a good idea to plan out what information it will contain, how many fields it will need, how the fields will be ordered, and how the fields will be used. Creating your database will be much easier after some basic planning, and you can avoid making changes later.

Database entries are no different from any other 1-2-3 entry. You can change formatting, move and copy, print, edit, and so on.

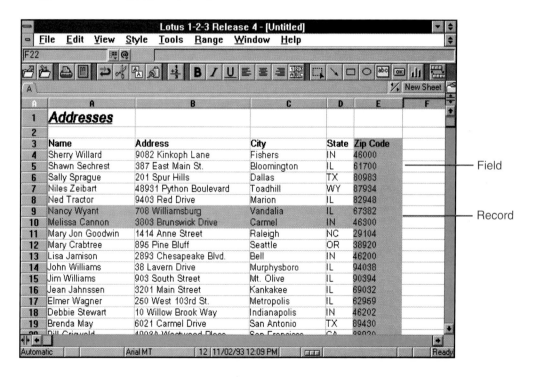

123

CREATING A DATABASE

Creating a Database

1 Enter the field names in the first row of the database table.

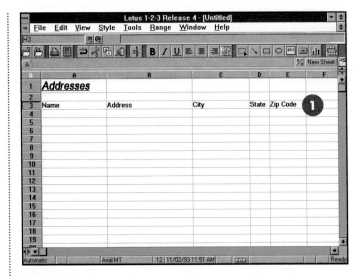

2 Enter the data for the first record in the second row of the table.

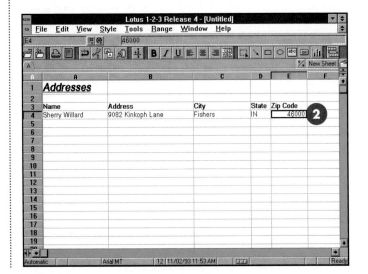

CREATING A DATABASE

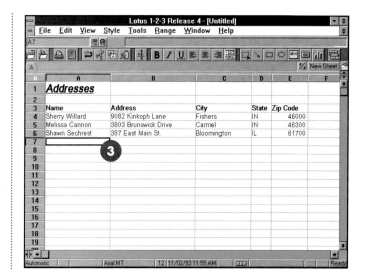

③ Continue to enter records in the subsequent rows. Apply formatting as needed.

TIP

No Blank Rows Allowed! Database tables cannot contain any blank rows. Records may have blank fields (cells) but never an entire blank row.

Beyond the Basics

SORTING A DATABASE

Why Sort a Database?

One major reason for creating a database is so you can sort records into a particular order. For example, if you were working with a database of names and addresses, you might want to sort the records by city, state, or zip code. 1-2-3 helps you sort your records based on these specific fields. A field specified to sort by is called a *sort key*.

Always use at least one sort key to keep your database records in some kind of order. If the sort key is a value field, your records will be sorted into numerical order. If the sort key is a label, your records will be sorted by alphabet letter or number.

When more than one record contains identical sort keys, you can specify additional ascending and descending sort keys to determine the order within that key. When the database is sorted, 1-2-3 displays the records in the new order.

Sorting a Database

1 Highlight the worksheet range that includes the database records *but not the field names*.

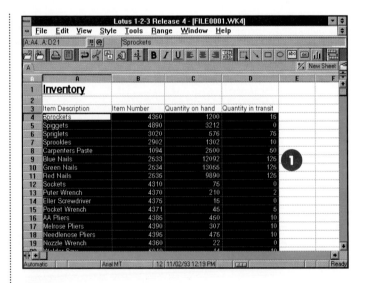

2 Select **Range**, or press **Alt+R**.

3 Select **Sort**, or press **S**.

4 When the Sort dialog box
appears, enter the cell address
that contains the field you want
the records sorted by in the
Sort by text box.

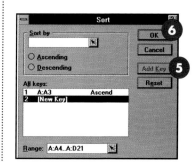

5 If desired, click on the Add **K**ey
button to add more (or secon-
dary) sort keys to your database
sort. Specify the cell addresses
of any additional sort keys in
the secondary sort key field.

6 Click on **OK**, or press **Enter** to
start the sort.

TIP

Clear Old Sort Keys   You can quickly clear all sort keys you've defined by clicking on the
Reset button in the Sort dialog box

Beyond the Basics

SEARCHING A DATABASE

Why Search a Database?

Another reason to create a database is so you can search for specific records. You may perform this task quite often. For example, if you're working with an address database, you might need to locate all the addresses in Illinois. A search for specific information is called a *query*. In the above example, STATE=IL is a criterion in the search. In order to perform a query, you must specify the exact criteria you are looking for.

1-2-3 recognizes certain operator symbols, such as = in the previous example, that tell 1-2-3 how to compare the data in the database. If you use more than one criterion in a query, you must tell 1-2-3 how to combine them in the search. When you perform a query, you must tell 1-2-3 what the range of the search is, what criteria are to be met, and where the results should appear. Once this information is defined, 1-2-3 searches the database to see whether or not each record meets the criteria you designated.

Operator Symbol	Meaning
=	equal to
< >	not equal to
>	greater than
<	less than
< =	less than or equal to
> =	greater than or equal to

TIP

AND and OR Connectors   If you instruct 1-2-3 to use more than one criterion in a query, you must also tell 1-2-3 how to combine them. If you select two criteria, for example, you must tell 1-2-3 whether a record must meet both the criteria to be considered a "match," or if one is sufficient. The AND and OR connectors help with this dilemma. If two criteria are connected with an AND, the record is considered a match only if it meets both. If two criteria are connected with an OR, a record is considered a match if it meets either one or both of the criteria.

Performing a Query

1 Highlight the entire database, including field names in the first row.

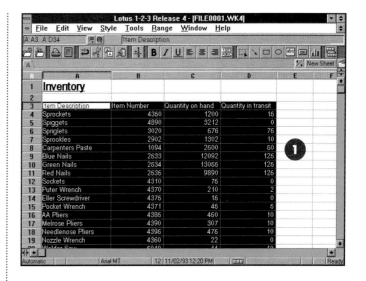

2 Click on Tools, or press **Alt+T**.

3 Click on Database, or press **B**.

4 Click on New Query, or press **N**.

5 In the New Query dialog box, click on Set Criteria, or press **Alt+C**.

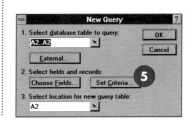

Beyond the Basics

6 Select **Clear** to delete any existing criteria in the Criteria list.

7 Select a field from the **Field** drop-down list.

8 Select an operator symbol from the **Op**erator drop-down list.

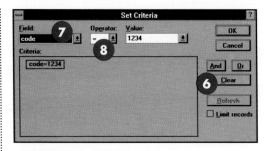

9 Enter the criterion in the **Value** box, or drop down the box to select from a list of values present.

10 Click the **And** or the **Or** button to enter additional criteria, and then repeat steps 7 through 9.

11 Select **OK**, or press **Enter**.

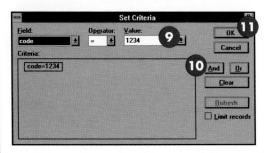

12 Enter the address where you want the results of the query inserted in the Select location for new **q**uery table box.

13 Select **OK**, or press **Enter.**

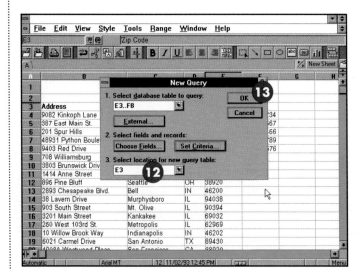

1-2-3 FOR WINDOWS INSTALLATION

Before you can use Lotus 1-2-3 to create and edit worksheets, the program must be installed on your computer. You will need the diskettes that came with the Lotus 1-2-3 for Windows package. These are either 3 1/2- or 5 1/4-inch diskettes that are labeled Disk 1, Disk 2, and so on. Once you have located the diskettes, you are ready to begin.

1 If necessary, turn on your computer and start Windows by typing **win**.

2 Place installation disk number one in your computer's diskette drive.

3 From the Program Manager screen, click on **File**, or press **Alt+F** to display the File menu.

4 Select **R**un from the **File** menu by clicking on **Run** or pressing **R**. This will display the Run dialog box.

5 In the Command Line text box type **a:install** (if you placed the diskette in drive A:) or **b:install** (if you placed the diskette in drive B:), and then press **Enter** or click on **OK**.

6 The Welcome to Install dialog box appears. Click on **OK**, or press **Enter**.

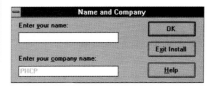

7 When prompted, enter your name and appropriate organization. Click on **OK**, or press **Enter** when finished.

8 Another box will appear asking you to confirm the names you entered. Click **Yes**, or press **Enter** to continue.

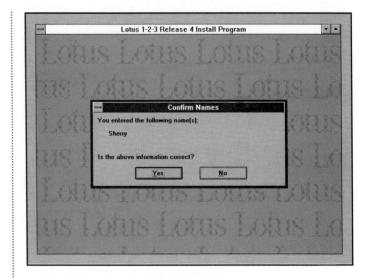

9 The Main Menu box will appear. Click on **Install 1-2-3**, or press **Enter**.

10 The next box gives you three installation options to choose from. Default Installation should work fine for you. Click on the button to the left of **Default Install**, or press **Enter**.

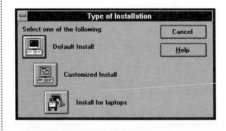

11 The 1-2-3 Directory dialog box lets you choose which drive and directory to install the program to. How much space is needed to install the program is also indicated. (The default directory is **123R4W**, which stands for 1-2-3 release 4.0 for Windows.) Once you've designated a directory, or if you're choosing the default directory, click on **OK**, or press **Enter**.

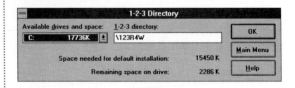

12 Another box appears asking you to confirm the directory you chose. Click on **Yes**, or press **Enter**.

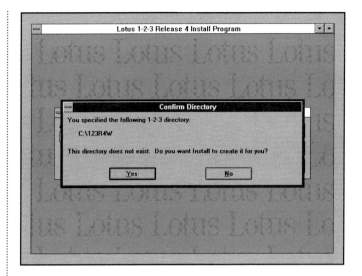

13 When the Lotus Common Directory box appears, in the **Lotus Common directory** text box, type in a program group name where you want 1-2-3 installed to, or use the default group name. When finished, click **OK**, or press **Enter**.

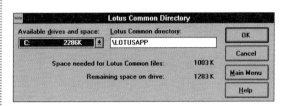

14 A confirmation box will appear again, asking you to confirm the directory you chose. Click on **Yes**, or press **Enter**.

The Install program will now begin copying the necessary files from the installation diskettes to your computer's hard disk. All you need to do is follow the instructions on-screen, changing diskettes when prompted.

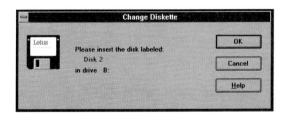

When the installation is complete, click on **OK**, or press **Enter** in the Installation Finished dialog box. A Take the Guided Tour box will appear. If you're interested in seeing an overview of the program, select **Yes**. If not, select **No**, and the Main Menu box shows up again. From here, you can exit the Install program and return to the Program Manager screen. You are now ready to run 1-2-3 for Windows.

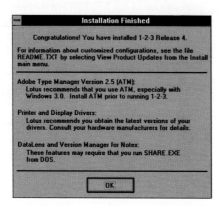

Glossary

absolute cell reference   An address or cell reference that specifies a fixed worksheet location.

active worksheet   The worksheet you are currently working on. It has a highlighted title bar. When more than one worksheet is opened, only one can be worked on at a time.

alignment   Positioning of data inside a cell.

applications   Programs that run on your computer, such as word processors, spreadsheets, databases, and graphics programs.

argument   Information that tells a 1-2-3 function how to manipulate or calculate data.

cell address   A worksheet cell location stated as a column letter and a row number. Also called a cell reference.

click   To tap or press the left mouse button.

Clipboard   A temporary storage area in the Windows software, which can be used by most Windows-based programs. You can put a selection into the Clipboard with the Cut or Copy commands, and retrieve the selection from the Clipboard with the Paste command.

commands   Orders that tell the computer what to do.

context-sensitive   A type of Help system that takes you directly to the information pertaining to the task you are trying to perform, without routing you through a topical index.

copy   To duplicate a section of data and insert it in a new location. You end up with two copies of the data, one in the original location and one in the new location.

database   An organized collection of data in a structured format.

dialog box   A box that appears when the program requires additional information from you to carry out a command.

directory   Special areas in your computer's hard disk where files are stored.

disk drive   A computer device that writes data to a magnetic disk and reads data from the disk.

DOS prompt   A set of characters (usually **C:\\>**) on the left side of the screen, followed by a blinking underline. DOS commands are typed in to the right of the DOS prompt.

double-click   To tap the left mouse button twice in rapid succession.

drag   To press and hold the mouse button while moving the mouse to a new location.

edit   To make changes in your data, or otherwise modify your worksheet.

ellipsis   Three dots, or periods, following a menu command, which indicate that a dialog box will appear when the command is selected.

existing worksheet file   A worksheet that has been saved previously.

file name   A name assigned to a worksheet stored on disk. You designate the first part of the name, up to 8 characters. 1-2-3 automatically adds the extension **.WK4** at the end of the file name.

file type   The format used to save the worksheet on disk. A file's type is identified by the three-character file name extension.

floppy disk   A small, portable magnetic disk used to save and store the data created on your computer.

GLOSSARY

floppy disk drive   A disk drive in your computer that uses floppy disks.

font   A set of characters with a specific design.

formatting   Changes made to the look of data, such as making it bolder and larger, or altering its position. Also called *attributes* or *enhancements*.

formula   An instruction that tells 1-2-3 to perform calculations on designated values.

frame   A special border used to emphasize worksheet data.

function   A built-in formula preset by 1-2-3 to handle common calculations. Also called *an @function*.

hard disk   A permanent disk drive located inside your computer. Hard disks hold more data than floppy disks.

highlight   A black or colored bar or border surrounding selected commands or data.

icon   A small picture on-screen that represents a program, an action you can take, or a piece of information.

insertion point   A short vertical line that marks the location in which text you type appears.

label prefix character   One of three special characters (' " and ^) that mark a cell entry as a label.

legend   A key that identifies a graph's data.

menu   A list of commands (or other choices) displayed in a drop-down box on your screen.

mouse   A hand-held device used to move the cursor or the highlighting around the computer screen in order to point at various program elements and to select them.

move   To change the location of a section of data on your worksheet, so you have only one copy of the data, in the new location.

operator   A mathematical symbol indicating an action, such as addition, subtraction, multiplication, division, and exponentiation, that 1-2-3 can perform on values.

operator precedence   The order in which 1-2-3 performs mathematical operations in a formula.

point   A measurement of character size and spacing. There are 72 points in an inch.

range   A rectangular area of one or more worksheet cells that are treated as one.

relative cell address   An address that specifies a worksheet location relative to the cell containing the formula.

selection letter   An underlined letter in the menu or command name. Keyboard users can choose the command or menu by holding down the **Alt** key and pressing the underlined selection letter.

shortcut key   A key, or combination of keys, you can use to issue a command without using the menus.

style   A collection of specifications for formatting text (for example, 12-point centered Arial label). A style may include information for the font, size, style, and number format. Applying a style to data automatically formats the data according to that style's specifications.

worksheet   A grid-like page in the 1-2-3 program where numeric values, formulas, and text data is entered.

Index

Symbols

$ (dollar sign)
    formulas, 58
( ) parentheses, operator precedence, 56
* (multiplication) operator, 55
+ (addition) operator, 55
- (subtraction) operator, 55
... (ellipsis), 135
/ (division) operator, 55
< (less than) operator symbol, 128
<= (less than or equal to) operator symbol, 128
<> (not equal to) operator symbol, 128
= (equals to) operator symbol, 128
> (greater than) operator symbol, 128
>= (greater than or equal to) operator symbol, 128
@Function List dialog box, 61
@function menu commands, List All, 61
@function selector, 60-61
@functions, 59-62, 136
^ (exponentiation) operator, 55
1-2-3 Directory dialog box, 132
3-D ranges, 48
3D charts, 103

A-B

absolute cell references, 57-58, 71-74, 135
active cell, 30
active worksheets, 135
addition (+) operator, 55
addresses of cells, 135
    ranges, 49
Align Left/Right Smarticons, 22
alignment, 135
    labels, 44
Alt key, 17-21
AND connector, 128
applications, 12, 135
arcs, 118-119
area charts, 103
arguments, 59, 135
arrows, 118-119
Automatic format, 85
axis, 105
    scales, 115-116
Axis command (Chart menu), 113-115
Axis dialog box, 115-116
Backspace key, 21, 68
Bad Command or Filename? error message, 12
bar charts, 103
Bold Smarticon, 22
borders, 95-97
built-in functions, see @functions

C

calendar @functions, 60
cell pointers, 30
cell references, 29-30, 71-74
    absolute, 57-58, 135
    relative, 57-58, 136

cells
    addresses, 135
    data
        copying/moving, 71-74
        deleting, 70
        editing, 69-70
    labels for charts, 114
    see also ranges
Center Smarticon, 22
changing, see editing
characters, label prefixes, 44, 136
Chart command (Tools menu), 104
Chart menu commands
    Axis, 113-115
    Headings, 111
    Legend, 112
charts, 102-105
    axis, 113-114
        scales, 115-116
    deleting, 106
    enhancements, 110
    footnotes, 111
    legends, 112
    moving, 107-109
    printing, 106
    resizing, 107-109
    rules, 106
    saving, 106
    titles, 111
check boxes, 21
circles, 119-120
Clear command (Edit menu), 70
Clear dialog box, 70
clicking with mouse 7, 14, 135
Clipboard, 23, 135
    data, copying/moving, 71-74
Close command (File menu), 77
Close dialog box, 77
Close Smarticon, 79
closing worksheets, 77
Column Width dialog box, 92
columns, 29-30
    width, 91-94
combo boxes, 21
Comma format, 85
command buttons, 20-21
commands, 15, 135
    @function menu, List All, 61
    Chart menu
        Axis, 113-115
        Headings, 111
        Legend, 112
    Edit menu
        Clear, 70
        Cut, 107
        Insert, 34
        Paste, 108
        Undo, 70
    ellipsis (...), 135
    File menu
        Close, 77
        Exit, 38
        New, 76
        Open, 75, 76
        Page Setup, 81-82
        Print, 80-82
        Print Preview, 78-79
        Save, 63-65
        Save As, 3, 63-65
    Help menu, 17-19
        Contents, 28
    Range menu
        Name, 50
        Sort, 126

Style menu
    Font & Attributes, 89
    Lines & Color, 96
    Named Style, 98-99
    Number Format, 86
    Worksheet Defaults, 90
Tools menu
    Chart, 104
    Database, New Query, 129
    Draw, 118-120
    Smarticons, 25-26
View menu
    Preferences, 26
    Split, 37
computers, 6
    keyboard, 8
    mouse, 7
    system unit, 7
connectors, AND/OR, 128
Contents command (Help menu), 28
context-sensitive Help, 27, 135
Control menu, 14-16
Copy Smarticon, 22, 74
copying, 135
    cells, 71-74
    worksheets, 71-74
Ctrl key, 71-74
Currency format, 85
cursor movement keys, worksheet window, 32
Cut command (Edit menu), 107
Cut Smarticon, 22, 74, 108

D

data, 40, 45
    editing, 68-70, 135
    formatting, 84-87
        borders, 95-97
        fonts, 88-90
        rows/columns, 91-94
        styles, 98-99
    labels, 40, 44
    values, 40, 43
    see also numbers; text
data entry, 40
    @functions, 60-61
    dates, 43
    formulas, 52-54
    labels, 42
    mistakes, correcting, 41
    times, 43
    values, 41
        entering as labels, 44
data series, charts, 102-103
database queries, 129
database @functions, 60
Database, New Query command (Tools menu), 129
databases, 123-125, 135
    queries, 128
    sorting, 126-127
Date and Time format, 85
date serial numbers, 43
dates, data entry, 43
decimals, formatting, 87
Delete key, 21, 68
deleting
    charts, 106
    data, 70
    names, ranges, 51
    worksheets, 35

dialog boxes, 20-21, 135
@Function List, 61
1-2-3 Directory, 132
Axis, 115-116
Clear, 70
Close, 77
Column Width, 92
Font & Attributes, 89
Headings, 111
Insert, 33-34
Installation Finished, 134
Legend, 110-112
Lines & Color, 95-97
Lotus Common Directory, 133
Name, 49-50
Named Style, 98-99
New Query, 129
Open, 75
Page Setup, 81-82
Print, 80-82
Print Preview, 78-79
Row Height, 93
Run, 131
Save As, 38
Smarticons, 25-26
Sort, 127
Split, 37
Type, 105
X-Axis, 114-116
Y-Axis, 114-116
directories, 8-9, 135
disk drives, 135
disks, 8-9
floppy, 9, 135
Display Smarticons Smarticon, 22
division (/) operator, 55
documents, see worksheets
dollar sign ($), formulas, 58
DOS prompt, 12, 135
double-clicking with mouse, 7, 14, 135
dragging mouse, 7, 135
Draw Arrow Smarticon, 22
Draw Circle/Ellipse Smarticon, 22
Draw command (Tools menu), 118-120
Draw Macro Button Smarticon, 22
Draw Square/Rectangle Smarticon, 22
Draw Text Box Smarticon, 22
drop-down list boxes, 21

E

Edit line, 15
Edit menu commands
Clear, 70
Cut, 107
Insert, 34
Paste, 108
Undo, 70
editing data, 68-70, 135
ellipsis (...), 17-18, 119, 135
engineering @functions, 60
entering data, see data entry
ERR message, formulas, 53
error messages
Bad Command or Filename?, 12
ERR, 53
Exit command (File menu), 38
exiting Lotus 1-2-3 for Windows, 38
exponentiation (^) operator, 55

F

F1 (Help) shortcut key, 28
fields, 123-125
file extensions, 63
File menu commands
Close, 77
Exit, 38
New, 76
Open, 75-76
Page Setup, 81-82
Print, 80-82
Print Preview, 78-79
Save, 63-65
Save As, 3, 63-65
files, 8-9, 63
names, 135
worksheet
adding worksheets, 33-34
deleting worksheets, 35
viewing multiple worksheets, 36-37
financial @functions, 60
Fixed format, 85
floppy disks, 9, 135
Font & Attributes command (Style menu), 89
Font & Attributes dialog box, 89
fonts, 85, 88-89, 136
default, 90
footers, 82
footnotes, charts/titles, 111
formatting data, 84-87, 136
borders, 95-97
fonts, 88-90
rows/columns, 91-94
styles, 98-99
formulas, 45, 52, 136
data entry, 52-54
dollar signs ($), 58
ERR message, 53
operator precedence, 55
parentheses, 56
frames, 136
Designer, 97
functions, 136
@functions, 59-62, 136
arguments, 59
categories, 60

G-J

General format, 85
Graph Smarticon, 22
graphic objects, 117-120
editing, 122

handles, objects, 122
hard disks, 9, 136
headers, 82
Headings command (Chart menu), 111
Headings dialog box, 111
Help, 27
context-sensitive, 135
Help button, 20-21
Help menu commands, Contents, 28
Hidden format, 85
hiding Smarticons, 24-26
Highlight bar, 17-18
highlighted icons/menu commands, 14, 136
HLCO (high-low-close-open) chart, 103

icons, 136
Lotus Applications, 13-14
information @functions, 60
Insert command (Edit menu), 34
Insert dialog box, 33-34
insertion point, 136
Installation Finished dialog box, 134
installing Lotus 1-2-3 for Windows, 131-134
Italic Smarticon, 22

K-L

keyboards, 8
keyboard shortcuts, 136
keys, cursor movement, worksheet window, 32
label prefix characters, 44, 136
labels, 40, 44-45
alignment, 44
cells for charts, 114
data entry, 42
Legend command (Chart menu), 112
Legend dialog box, 110-112
legends, 105, 112, 136
line charts, 103
lines, 118-119
Lines & Color command (Style menu), 96
Lines & Color dialog box, 95-97
List All command (@function menu), 61
list boxes, 20-21
logarithmic scale, axis, 114
logical @functions, 60
lookup @functions, 60
Lotus 1-2-3 for Windows 4.0, 1-2
exiting, 38
installing, 131-134
screen display, 2
starting, 13-14
Lotus Applications icon, 13-14
Lotus Common Directory dialog box, 133

M-N

mathematical @functions, 60
Maximize button, 16
measurement, see units of measurement
menus, 17-19, 136
messages, see error messages
Minimize button, 16
mixed charts, 103
moving, 136
cells/range of cells, 71-74
charts, 107-109
Smarticons, 24-26
worksheets, 71-74
multiple worksheets, 36-37
multiplication (*) operator, 55

Name command (Range menu), 50
Name dialog box, 49-50
Named Style command (Style menu), 98-99
Named Style dialog box, 98-99
New command (File menu), 76
New Query dialog box, 129
number boxes, 21
Number Format command (Style menu), 86
numbers
formatting, 86-87
see also data; text

O

objects, graphic, 117-122
on-screen Help, 27
Open command (File menu), 75-76
Open dialog box, 75
Open Smarticon, 22, 75
opening worksheets, 75-76
operator precedence, 55, 136
    parentheses, 56
operator symbols, 128
operators, 55-56, 136
option buttons, 21
OR connector, 128

P

Page Setup command (File menu), 81-82
Page Setup dialog box, 81-82
parentheses ( )
    operator precedence, 56
Paste command (Edit menu), 108
Paste Smarticon, 22, 74, 108
Percent format, 85
pie charts, 103
plot (charts), 105
point size, 88-89
pointers
    mouse, 31
pointing mouse, 7
pointing with mouse, 14
points (font measurement), 136
Preferences command (View menu), 26
Preview Smarticon, 79
Print command (File menu), 80-82
Print dialog box, 80-82
Print Preview command (File menu), 78-79
Print Preview dialog box, 78-79
Print Preview Smarticon, 22
Print Smarticon, 22, 79-80
printing
    charts, 106
    worksheets, 80-82
program group windows, Lotus Applications, 13-14
Program Manager, 13-14
    installing Lotus 1-2-3 for Windows, 131-132

Q-R

queries, 128-129
Quick menu, 18
quick saves, 65

radar charts, 103
Range menu commands
    Name, 50
    Sort, 126
range of cells
ranges, 46, 48, 136
    3-D, 48
    addresses, 49
    copying/moving, 71-74
    naming, 49-51
    selecting/deselecting, 47
    sorting, 126
records, 123-125
    sorting, 126-127

rectangles, 119
referencing cells
    absolute references, 57-58
    relative references, 57-58, 71-74, 136
resizing charts, 107-109
    see also sizing
right-clicking with mouse, 7
Row Height dialog box, 93
rows, 29-30
    height, 91-94
Run dialog box, 131

S

Save As command (File menu), 3, 63-65
Save As dialog box, 38
Save command (File menu), 63-65
Save Smarticon, 22
saving
    charts, 106
    worksheets, 3, 63-65
        directory location, 65
        quick saves, 65
scales, axis, 114-116
screen displays, Lotus 1-2-3 main screen, 2
screens, 15
scroll bars, 15
searches, *see* queries
Select Objects Smarticon, 22
selection letters
selection letters, menu commands, 17-19, 136
Sequence in Selected Range Smarticon, 22
serial date numbers, 43
shortcut keys, 17-19
    cutting/copying/pasting, 74
sizing charts, 104
    see also resizing
Smarticons, 15, 22
    Close, 79
    Copy, 74
    Cut, 74, 108
    graphics drawing commands, 119
    moving/hiding, 24-26
    Open, 75
    Paste, 108
    Preview, 79
    Print, 79-80
    sets, 23
    Undo, 70
Smarticons command (Tools menu), 25-26
Smarticons dialog box, 25-26
Sort command (Range menu), 126
Sort dialog box, 127
sort keys, 126-127
Split command (View menu), 37
Split dialog box, 37
standard scale, axis, 114
starting
    Lotus 1-2-3 for Windows, 13-14
    Windows, 12
statistical @functions, 60
Status bar, 15
Style menu commands
    Font & Attributes, 89
    Lines & Color, 96
    Named Style, 98-99
    Number Format, 86
    Worksheet Defaults, 90
styles, 98-99, 136

submenus, 17-18
subtraction (-) operator, 55
Sum Smarticon, 22
Synchronized Scrolling option, 37
system unit (computers), 7

T-V

Tab key, 20-21
Table of Contents, Help, 27-28
text @functions, 60
text blocks, 120-121
    see also data; numbers
text boxes, 20-21
Text format, 85
time, data entry, 43
Title bar, 15
Tools menu commands
    Chart, 104
    Database, New Query, 129
    Draw, 118-120
    Smarticons, 25-26
transparent graphic objects, 122
Type dialog box, 105

undeleting data entry errors, 41
Underline Smarticon, 22
Undo command (Edit menu), 70
Undo Smarticon, 22, 70
unit titles, charts, 114
units of measurement, points, 136

values, 40-45
View menu commands.
    Preferences, 26
    Split, 37
viewing worksheets, multiple, 36-37

W-Z

Windows, starting, 12
work area, screens, 15
Worksheet Defaults command (Style menu), 90
worksheet window, navigating, 29-31
    cursor movement keys, 32
    navigating, 31
worksheets, 14, 30, 136
    active, 135
    adding to files, 33-34
    cells, labels, 114
    closing, 77
    copying, 71-74
    deleting, 35
    moving, 71-74
    names, 64
    opening, 75-76
    Print Preview, 78-79
    printing, 80-82
    saving, 3, 63-65
        directory location, 65
        quick saves, 65
    viewing multiple, 36-37

X-Axis dialog box, 114, 116
XY charts, 103

Y-Axis dialog box, 114, 116

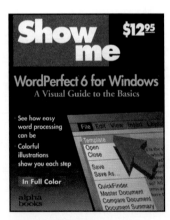